30119 024 566 475

WPK

09/07

LOST RAILWAYS
OF SURREY

Leslie Oppitz

COUNTRYSIDE BOOKS

NEWBURY BERKSHIRE

D1081134

First published 2002
© Leslie Oppitz 2002

Reprinted 2005

All rights reserved. No reproduction
permitted without the prior permission
of the publisher:

COUNTRYSIDE BOOKS
3 Catherine Road
Newbury, Berkshire

To view our complete range of books,
please visit us at
www.countrysidebooks.co.uk

ISBN 1 85306 771 7

The cover picture shows Schools class locomotive *Stowe* 4-4-0
no 30928 hauls a Hastings bound express travelling southwards
towards Redhill in the late 1950s. The train was probably diverted via
the Redhill-Tonbridge line following repair work in Sevenoaks tunnel.
Stowe was built at Eastleigh in 1934 and withdrawn in 1962. (From
original painting by Colin Doggett)

Maps by Jennie Collins and Brian Butler

Produced through MRM Associates Ltd., Reading
Printed by Woolnough Bookbinding Ltd., Irthlingborough

CONTENTS

LONDON BOROUGH OF SUTTON LIBRARY SERVICE	
024566475	
Askews	Sep-2007
625	

ABBREVIATIONS

The following abbreviations are used in this book:

CM&G	Croydon, Merstham & Godstone Iron Railway
CO&EGR	Croydon, Oxted & East Grinstead Railway
GER	Great Eastern Railway
GWR	Great Western Railway
L&BR	London & Brighton Railway
L&CR	London & Croydon Railway
L&GR	London & Greenwich Railway
LBSCR	London, Brighton & South Coast Railway (an amalgamation of the L&CR and L&BR from 1846)
LCDR	London, Chatham & Dover Railway
LCGB	Locomotive Club of Great Britain
LNC	London Necropolis Company
LNER	London & North Eastern Railway
LNWR	London & North Western Railway
LSWR	London & South Western Railway
M&TVR	Metropolitan & Thames Valley Railway
RCTS	Railway Correspondence and Travel Society
S&SJR	Surrey & Sussex Junction Railway
SCTS	Southern Counties Touring Society
SECR	South Eastern & Chatham Railway (the working union of the SER & LCDR from 1899)
SER	South Eastern Railway
SIR	Surrey Iron Railway

Please note that:
'Junction' implies a railway station
'junction' means where railway lines meet

5

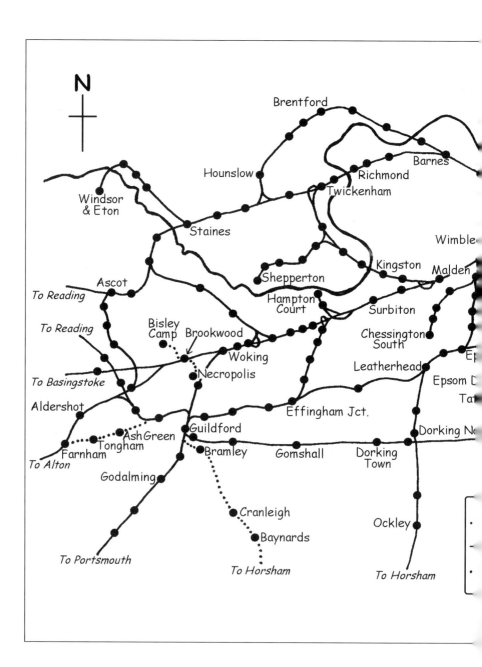

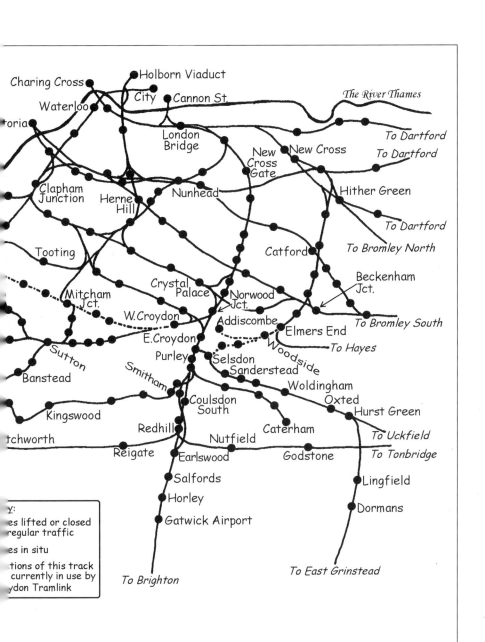

Charing Cross
Holborn Viaduct
City
Cannon St.
Waterloo
The River Thames
-toria
London
Bridge
New
Cross
Gate
New Cross
To Dartford
To Dartford
Clapham
Junction
Herne
Hill
Nunhead
Hither Green
To Dartford
Tooting
Catford
To Bromley North
Crystal
Palace
Norwood
Jct.
Beckenham
Jct.
Mitcham
Jct.
W. Croydon
Addiscombe
To Bromley South
E. Croydon
Elmers End
To Hayes
Purley
Woodside
Sutton
Selsdon
Banstead
Smitham
Sanderstead
Woldingham
Oxted
Kingswood
Coulsdon
South
Caterham
Hurst Green
Redhill
Nutfield
To Uckfield
-tchworth
Reigate
Earlswood
Godstone
To Tonbridge
Salfords
Lingfield
Horley
Dormans
Gatwick Airport
To Brighton
To East Grinstead

-y:
-es lifted or closed
-regular traffic

-es in situ

-tions of this track
 currently in use by
-ydon Tramlink

ACKNOWLEDGEMENTS

Thanks are due to the many libraries throughout Surrey who have given valuable assistance during the research of this book. Thanks also go to the late J.L. Smith of Lens of Sutton whose patience in the 1980s enabled me to acquire numerous early photographs, many of which were used in my earlier publication *Surrey Railways Remembered*.

Acknowledgements are due to the *Croydon Advertiser* Group of Newspapers for its encouragement in the late 1980s when publishing many of my early railway articles which together later formed the basis of this book. Also thanks to the numerous *Oakwood Press* publications whose in-depth studies gave valuable guidance where previously very little material had been available.

Personal thanks go to John H. Meredith of York and Arthur Tayler C.Eng F.I.Mech.E of Betchworth, Surrey. Thanks also to John Bradshaw of Sanderstead, Surrey, Anthony Rispoli, railway photographer and Stephen Parascandolo for their invaluable input of information and photographs. Also to Brian Butler of Burgess Hill who produced the original maps and to Muriel, my sister, who helped with checking.

Finally thanks go to my wife Joan who gave considerable assistance and encouragement and also proved herself once again to be a capable assistant and proof reader!

Introduction

At the start of the 19th century no railways existed in Southern England. Passenger travel and movement of freight was by road, canal or by coastal vessels. In Surrey one of the first turnpikes was a trust established in 1696 covering a road from Reigate to Crawley in Sussex. More were to follow and by 1770 a turnpike was established from London to Brighton. Canals had been dug in the early 1800s adding to the rivers already made navigable but transport was slow and none of these ventures was financially successful.

In the opening years of the 19th century, Britain was at war with Napoleon and it was the need to divert vessels from the perilous Dover Straits that brought about a scheme to link the important naval base of Portsmouth with London. When France was defeated at Trafalgar in 1805 the danger to Channel shipping lessened but the need for such a commercial link remained.

It was in this climate that the world's first public railway came into existence. Intended to reach Portsmouth from the capital, there was a proposal to open a route, partly by rail and partly by canal. Initially the first section from the Thames at Wandsworth was to have been canal but it was decided that such a move would be harmful to the industries of the Wandle valley. Instead the 8 mile long Surrey Iron Railway from Wandsworth to Croydon was built. Within two years the Croydon, Merstham & Godstone Iron Railway had linked Croydon with lime quarries at Merstham.

Activities now moved northwards following George Stephenson's enthusiasm over locomotive engines. With the opening of the Stockton to Darlington Railway in 1825, the first steam train had arrived. In the same year an Act was granted for the Canterbury & Whitstable Railway to be built. In 1826 a line between Liverpool and Manchester was approved and three years later the famous Rainhill trials took place to establish which type of steam locomotive would give the best means of traction.

Travelling was pretty uncomfortable in those early days. Railway carriages began as stagecoach bodies attached to wagon bases. They were small, cramped and unlit and had no heating or travel facilities. When lighting came it was by oil lamps, subsequently to be replaced by gas lamps. Steam heating and comfortable seating came late in the century and the 1880s saw the introduction of dining cars with equipped kitchens, purpose-built for long distance travel. It is a sad reflection that the luxuries of Pullman car travel are today almost defunct!

In 1836 the London & Croydon Railway purchased the failing Croydon Canal for £40,250. Construction of the railway pushed ahead quickly, much of it along the old canal bed. The line was completed in 1839. A rail route southwards to Brighton was already under consideration and it was a proposal submitted by Sir John Rennie that was finally adopted. By the 1840s railway lines were spreading rapidly across the county. Because of competition, the canals had no hope and all were to be abandoned commercially by the end of the 1800s.

Despite improving roadway systems, it became quicker and easier to move freight by rail. Freight depots were built and goods traffic became a feature at almost every station. Few stations, however small, were without a number of sidings as business continued to increase. Truly the railways had arrived!

In more recent times, Surrey remains unique in the south east of England since, during the extensive cuts of the 1950s and 1960s, very few lines were affected. In fact, most of the lines north of the old South Eastern Railway (SER) route from Tonbridge in Kent to Reading in Berkshire remain relatively untouched.

In writing *Lost Railways of Surrey* therefore, the emphasis is on the lines as they were, from their early origins to their usage since their opening. Several lines have of course disappeared such as the Necropolis branch and Bisley Camp branch, both leaving the main line at Brookwood, near Woking. The Horsham to Guildford branch closed in 1965 and the short route through Ash Green and Tongham (near Aldershot) was closed to passengers in July 1937. The stretch from Woodside to Selsdon was abandoned in May 1983. In May 1997 the line between West Croydon and Wimbledon and also the short branch to

10

Addiscombe closed so that construction work could be begin on today's Croydon Tramlink system.

From the early days of the Surrey Iron Railway at the beginning of the 19th century, the book takes the reader through the early struggles over routes southwards from London Bridge including the battles in 1839 between the London & Greenwich Railway and the London & Croydon Railway to gain access to London Bridge station. Subsequently it follows the experimental days of atmospheric trains ('Trains that ran on Air!') and then on to early ideas of electric trains from the year 1901 when there were plans for a monorail system from London to Brighton.

The ensuing chapters include many major routes and branch lines of historical interest. Highlighted are details of the many bitter battles between the different railway companies. In the east the London, Brighton & South Coast Railway (LBSCR) and the SER had many serious disputes over territories. At one stage these appeared resolved by an 1848 agreement, but the troubles went on for many years. To the west the LBSCR and the London & South Western Railway (LSWR) had frequent problems, culminating at one stage in December 1858 when a Guildford train became involved in the famous 'Battle of Havant'.

For the sake of historical background the earlier county borders of Surrey (before the 1965 changes) have been taken into consideration. Also, to include the earlier Gatwick days, the Local Government reorganisation of 1974 which placed Gatwick in West Sussex has been disregarded.

Leslie Oppitz

1
An Iron Railway Reaches Merstham

Throughout the centuries Croydon has been a thriving market town of some importance. For a lengthy period, it was bounded by large areas of forest in which the practice of charcoal-burning developed. At that time, charcoal, then commonly known as 'coal', provided fuel for domestic heating. With London needing such supplies for its own requirements, and the many banquets of the day, it was becoming increasingly necessary to introduce an improved transportation system. The roads were generally poor, usually rutted or potted, and frequently thick with mud in poor weather.

It was not until the beginning of the 19th century that a decision was taken by local industrialists to promote a railway from the Thames at Wandsworth to Croydon, and later beyond, although earlier a canal had been envisaged. The canal idea was dropped since it would have proved detrimental to the river-based industries which utilised mills and works dependent on the river to provide their power.

An Act agreeing to the construction of the Surrey Iron Railway (SIR) was agreed by Parliament on 21st May 1801 and the subsequent Croydon, Merstham & Godstone Iron Railway on 17th May 1803. The SIR, to be used for the pulling of freight, was to become the first such public railway in the world. The eight miles of track from Wandsworth to Croydon officially opened on 26th July 1803. Horses, donkeys or mules pulled four-wheeled wagons, transported either singly or coupled into trains. Their loads included coal, iron, copper, bricks, grain and oilseeds.

The track was mostly double, using plate rails mounted on stone blocks. There was a space of 4 ft 2 ins between the upturned flanges which guided the wagons' wheels. The section was available to the public on payment of a toll, which permitted merchants or carriers to use their own wagons or horses. There is no record of passenger services on the Iron Railway on a regular basis but it is quite possible that wagons were cleaned out and sometimes used for excursions or organised outings.

Little evidence remains today of this pioneer route. The terminus at Wandsworth was formerly a canal basin in the area of the river Wandle, Armoury Way and Fairfield Street. From here the track struck south to Summerstown, crossing where a railway line today exists at Earlsfield. From the west side of Lambeth Cemetery the track continued along Mead Path and near Grove Road to the present Colliers Wood station. Here the charcoal burners of the past are remembered since they were known as 'colliers'.

After passing along part of Church Road and crossing Baron Walk, the line met the (present-day) A217 at Mitcham station. From here the original railway crossed Mitcham Common following a south-easterly direction to West Croydon, much of it along the course of today's Wimbledon to Croydon tramway.

The Croydon terminus was finally reached at an area known as Reeves Corner where Tamworth Road, Cairo New Road and Church Road meet. From this terminus a separate iron railway was built to link the SIR terminus with the basin of the Croydon Canal not far away. Not far from today's West Croydon railway station once stood 132, Waddon New Road, considered to be a tollhouse for the SIR. A bricked-up window suggested this was where tolls from passing wagons were collected. But later research suggests this property was built around 1852 for use with a coal depot and siding.

In June 1804 a short SIR branch line opened from Mitcham (Willow Lane Bridge) to Hackbridge. The track bore southwards for one and a quarter miles to follow the London Road (A237) past the Skinners Arms then curving to follow Hackbridge Road before crossing Hack Bridge. The original bridge of cast iron segments was demolished in 1912 and has since twice been replaced, the last time in 1983. The trains terminated close to the Wandle and opposite the site of Shepley Mills, just north of the present Carshalton to Hackbridge line.

13

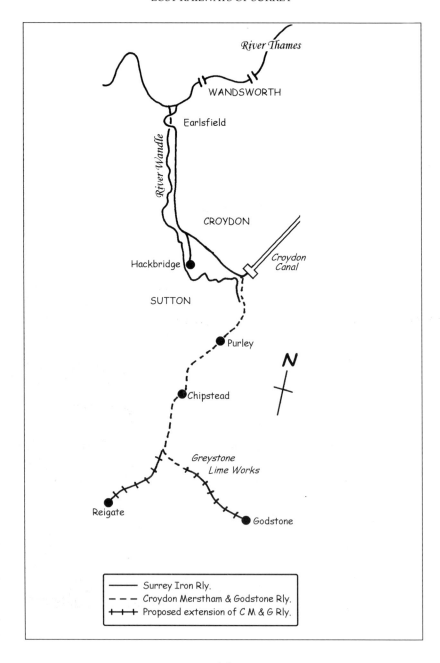

The mills were probably once used for fulling wool but by the late 17th century they were manufacturing gunpowder. There were four mills although by 1744 three had become copper mills, rolling out copper sheet. The fourth was used for grinding dyewoods but this was converted to an oil mill which was later served by a siding from the Iron Railway where wagons brought in supplies of oilseeds.

The Hackbridge branch is said to have survived until 1846 by which time the conventional railways were taking over. Little evidence remains of the old line. The many stone sleeper blocks used in The Grove, Carshalton probably came from the Shepley Mills area but the rails that have been displayed for many years outside Wallington Library apparently came from stone mines at Godstone.

Much of the Croydon, Merstham & Godstone Iron Railway (CM&G) was single track although it was doubled for at least part of its existence. It opened officially in July 1805, with its terminus at the Croydon end forming an end-on junction with the Surrey Iron Railway from Wandsworth. The CM&G was originally intended to include a 'main line' to Reigate as the first

Remains of an overbridge and abutment used on the Croydon, Merstham & Godstone Iron Railway at Hooley. (Author)

15

A preserved section of track from the Godstone mines can be found opposite the Feathers at Merstham. (Author)

stage of an extension to Portsmouth but the subsequent victory by Nelson at Trafalgar removed the French threat to Channel shipping and there was no further need. The line eventually only reached the stone mines at Quarry Dean, Merstham. Typical loads included chalk, lime, Fuller's Earth, timber and firestone.

On 15th July 1837 an Act was passed whereby the London & Brighton Railway was authorised to purchase the CM&G line. With the advent of conventional railways, the CM&G had no further use. The sale was completed by the end of 1838 and by an Act passed on 1st July 1839 the Croydon, Merstham & Godstone Railway Company was dissolved.

No real trace of the CM&G remains through Croydon but the line existed along Tramway Road (now called Church Road). From close to the A23 at the Swan and Sugar Loaf, South Croydon, it passed across Haling Park to follow west of the Brighton Road through to Purley. At the Rotary Field a short length of track been preserved in a railed-off area. The centre path across the field is noticeably terraced, being part of the original permanent way.

16

The Croydon, Merstham & Godstone Iron Railway closed in 1839. The southern end between Hooley and Merstham was located where today the M23 exists. (Author)

Chipstead Valley was crossed by an overbridge. There is no evidence of this today but part of the embankment has survived and can be located close to an Elim Chapel. After passing through the grounds of Cane Hill Hospital (the hospital was built subsequently in 1883), the line crossed the A23 at the junction of Hollymeoak Road and Woodplace Lane. Further south at Hooley, certain of the houses built on the east side of the A23 were constructed on surplus earth from the necessary railway cuttings.

Clear evidence of a brick parapet and abutments of an over-bridge can be seen from the A23 (just before the M23 turn-off) on the north side of Dean Lane. Unfortunately for posterity, the motorway has destroyed much of the remaining evidence but by staying on the old A23 one passes a deep overgrown cutting which has existed for many years opposite Harps Oak Lane. There is a further reminder to be found opposite the Feathers at Merstham. In a small garden area across the road, rails exist (taken from the Godstone mines) although these do not represent the true track route.

With the Croydon Canal closing in 1836 and with eventual competition from steam trains, it was inevitable that these early railways should lose business. In 1837 the London & Brighton Railway (L&BR) required two stretches of the CM&G south of Coulsdon for its new line to the coast but by the Act dated 15th July 1837, the L&BR was required to purchase the whole company. In September 1838, the L&BR agreed to pay £9,614. 8s 0d to the CM&G plus £1,000 to compensate for loss of profits. With business almost at a standstill, the latter could indeed be considered generous! The CM&G was wound up in July 1839 although it may have been 1842 before the bulk of the track was removed.

Traffic on the SIR from Wandsworth to Croydon came to an end on 31st August 1846. The company's terminus at Croydon was sold to the Croydon and Epsom Railway but the transaction was delayed since it was found that the SIR had never paid for it in the first place! This was later resolved with the sale going through to the London, Brighton & South Coast Railway (LBSCR) which had meantime taken over the Croydon and Epsom company. The remaining land between Croydon and Mitcham, owned by the SIR, was subsequently sold to adjacent landowners and the Wandsworth dock area was sold by auction.

But this was still not the end. In 1853 a branch line from West Croydon to Wimbledon was authorised by Parliament and by 1855 conventional trains were using the original SIR route between Waddon Marsh and Mitcham. In order to do this, the railway company had to buy back the sections of trackbed that the SIR had sold. Now even the conventional trains have gone. Today smart new tramcars cover the route – part of the Croydon Tramlink system.

2
Croydon And A Line To Wimbledon

A late 1930s picture of East Croydon. SR no 2039 hauls a goods set; on the right is no 7755, the LMS (ex-LNWR) Webb 0-6-2 'Coal Tank' built in 1884. (Lens of Sutton)

Parliament agreed to the construction of a canal linking the Thames at Rotherhithe with Croydon in 1801, in the same year that the Surrey Iron Railway had been approved. The canal took many years to build and final completion was not until October 1809. The total cost amounted to £127,000 and throughout its 9¼ miles length, some 28 locks were necessary.

The Croydon Canal, as it became known, had little success and shareholders had no return for their money. It had been necessary to build reservoirs at Sydenham and South Norwood

A passenger train bound for Brighton and Eastbourne hauled by tank locomotive 80082 arrives at East Croydon station in 1956. (Arthur Tayler)

and also a pumping station at Croydon to maintain water levels. Despite this, leakages often left the canal short of water.

In 1834 Joseph Gibbs carried out a survey for a new railway line from London to Croydon which could make use of sections of the canal bed. His report was accepted by the board of the proposed London & Croydon Railway (L&CR) which made an immediate offer for the canal's purchase. The offer was rejected and it was not until 1836, after settlement by a jury, that a figure of £40,250 was agreed. Navigation on the canal ceased in August of that year.

The L&CR immediately went ahead with construction, building much of the track from Anerley to West Croydon (opened as 'Croydon') along the old canal bed. The station at West Croydon was built on the site of the canal basin and warehouses.

By the time the line opened on 5th June 1839, complications had arisen. One of these was the need to share London Bridge station with another company, the London and Greenwich Railway (L&GR). In consequence it was necessary to pay tolls to the L&GR per passenger when using their lines between Corbetts

20

junction (north of New Cross Gate station) and London Bridge. This was unavoidable since the L&CR's terminus was the wrong side of the L&GR's station at London Bridge.

To this day London Bridge remains broken into different sections as dictated by the early railway planning. Eventually in 1840 the companies agreed to exchange buildings since the toll system was needlessly complicated to operate. To carry this out, the original Greenwich-owned station, it was apparently a crude affair, required considerable enlargement. This was completed in 1842 at the expense of the L&CR and also the South Eastern Railway (SER) and the London & Brighton Railway (L&BR) which were now using the terminus. The stations were finally exchanged in 1844. At the southern end of the L&CR line, the Croydon company's offices were based at where West Croydon station is located today.

Some remaining difficulties at London Bridge were simplified when, in 1845, the SER took over the Greenwich Railway. This was coupled with proposals that the lines into the terminus should be widened to avoid further hostilities. But battles and complications continued.

The L&BR was soon unhappy with dependence on the L&CR for access to London and considered the building of an independent line to Vauxhall in an involvement with yet another company, the London & South Western Railway (LSWR). Meantime the L&CR and the SER joined forces to construct a new branch to a terminus at Bricklayer's Arms (named after a local hostelry and close to New Cross Gate) and invited the L&BR to participate. The station was called 'West End Terminus' because it was considered that access to the West End was easier from the new station than from London Bridge.

The venture proved disastrous. The L&BR turned down the offer, still being interested in an involvement with the LSWR. The new station at Bricklayer's Arms opened on 1st May 1844, but it was not to last. The L&CR withdrew its trains on 31st March 1845, and only half the SER trains now used the new terminus. The station finally closed to passengers in 1852 but remains a goods station to this day.

Bitter feelings remained between the L&CR and L&BR companies and it was reported that the latter gave instructions

21

Double track was built at Central Croydon with the terminus consisting of two side platforms plus numerous sidings. The platform buildings were constructed beyond the track area since there were no intentions of extending the line. (Lens of Sutton)

Central Croydon station at Katherine Street which opened in January 1868 to give passengers closer access to the town's shops. The idea was not successful and the station finally closed in August 1890. (Lens of Sutton)

LONDON BRIGHTON & SOUTH COAST RAILWAY

SEPTEMBER TRAIN SERVICE, 1890.

CLOSING OF CENTRAL CROYDON STATION

On and from Monday, September 1st, 1890, THE

CENTRAL CROYDON STATION

will be entirely closed, and at the same time the Trains now running to and from Central Croydon will not be continued beyond New Croydon, to and from which latter Station the same service of London Brighton and South Coast, London and North Western, and Great Eastern Companies' Trains, will still be given exactly as shown in the Time Books and Time Bills in force up to and including September 30th, 1890.

A notice of September 1890 announces the closure of Central Croydon station. (Lens of Sutton)

23

Looking south from East Croydon's main up platform on 26th March 1959.
On the left locomotive 0-6-0 class 01 no 31048 hauls a goods set.
(John H. Meredith)

Locomotive 34089 '602 Squadron' runs round an SCTS special train at
West Croydon on 5th June 1966. (John H. Meredith)

A tram picks up passengers at East Croydon railway station. Croydon Tramlink opened to the public on 10th May 2000 with a service between Croydon and New Addington. Later that month routes opened to Beckenham Junction and to Wimbledon. (Anthony Rispoli)

Earlier times when a Croydon Corporation car no 22 in George Street, Croydon makes for Addiscombe via East Croydon station, c1902. (Pamlin Prints)

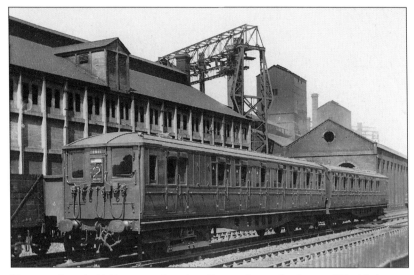

Two-coach unit 1811 passes Croydon Gasworks on the former Wimbledon to West Croydon line on 16th June 1951. (John H. Meredith)

that if any L&CR trains were waiting at the Jolly Sailor station (Norwood Junction) then they should be reversed into sidings to give any L&BR train priority! Meantime the arguments between the L&CR and L&BR companies continued. It was only when the L&BR planned another route to London via Wandsworth that the L&CR's hand was forced. Eventually the two agreed to amalgamate and in July 1846 the London, Brighton & South Coast Railway (LBSCR) was created.

On 22nd October 1855 a line opened jointly between the LBSCR and the LSWR between West Croydon and Wimbledon, part of the route previously used by the Surrey Iron Railway. On 1st January 1866 the LBSCR acquired full ownership. By the early 1920s there were 14 trains each way daily with less on Sundays. The line skirted Wandle Park towards Mitcham Junction, crossed the Streatham to Sutton line and finished at Wimbledon.

In January 1868 Croydon acquired a fourth railway station. West Croydon had long since been established and East Croydon had opened when the LBSCR had commenced services

An early picture of Waddon Marsh station photographed on 29th August 1953. On the right two gasworks locomotives. (John H. Meredith)

Today's Waddon Marsh station is used by Croydon Tramlink. The route from Elmers End to Wimbledon opened on 29th May 2000. (John H. Meredith)

A two-coach electric unit passes between Waddon Marsh and Beddington Lane on 9th April 1949. In the distance can be determined Croydon Airport wireless station masts. On the right Nelsons Factory, centre picture BR steelworks yard and to the left Cement Marketing Company sidings. (John H. Meredith)

Beddington Lane Halt on 30th April 1950, looking south-east. A linesman works on a telegraph pole where lines have fallen across the bushes on the left following a blizzard on 25th/26th April 1950. (John H. Meredith)

Units 1810 and 1811 approach Mitcham from Wimbledon in bank holiday formation on Whit-Monday 6th June 1949. (John H. Meredith)

The former Merton Abbey station between Tooting Junction and Merton Park photographed 7th April 1950. Merton Abbey closed to passenger traffic on 2nd March 1929. (John H. Meredith)

to Haywards Heath in July 1841. South Croydon had opened in 1865. The new fourth station, initially called 'Central Croydon', was built by the LBSCR with much encouragement from the local Council. It was constructed as a short spur from East Croydon (then called 'New Croydon') passing under Park Lane to reach Catherine Street (as it was then spelt). Plans were in hand to discontinue Croydon Fair after 1867 (held each year since 1276) and this meant that Fair Field had become available for railway use. The station opened on 1st January 1868. Double track was built with the terminus consisting of two side platforms plus numerous sidings. The platform buildings were constructed beyond the track area since there were no intentions of extending the line.

The object of the short branch was to give closer access to the shops but, with New Croydon not far away, it did not prove successful. Consequently the service was withdrawn on 1st December 1871, although the actual line and station remained and may well have been used as sidings. As commercial activity grew in Croydon there was another move by the Croydon

A Southern Counties Touring Society special 'The South Londoner' at Merton Abbey on 20th April 1958. (John H. Meredith)

Council to provide a passenger train service to the shops. In consequence the station was refurbished and a service restarted on 1st June 1886.

When reopened, some records say its name had been changed to 'Croydon Central' but further research does not support this. Initially a number of London & North Western Railway (LNWR) trains used the station, running via Crystal Palace to and from Willesden Junction. In the following year Great Eastern Railway (GER) trains used Central Croydon via the East London line to and from Liverpool Street. Despite these efforts the station was never a success and in August 1890 the LBSCR was given powers to close the line. The site of the station and the surrounding land were sold to the Croydon Corporation which erected a replacement town hall and public gardens on the site.

Today trains no longer run to and from West Croydon and Wimbledon with the track having been taken over by Croydon Tramlink. The last train to cover the route ran on 31st May 1997. It was a Railtour Special comprising two Network SouthEast coaches class 423/1 4-VEP units 3543 and 3544. The train carried headboards reading L.I.L.O. (Last In Last Out). It was also the last train to work the Addiscombe branch (see Chapter 11). Passengers today probably little realise as they look out from the modern Tramlink cars that over part of their journey between Wimbledon and West Croydon they are retracing the route taken by the Surrey Iron Railway (the world's first public railway) 200 years ago!

3
'Atmospheric Trains'
That Ran On Air!

Pipes from the atmospheric railway dug out in 1933 not far from West Croydon station. (Photograph courtesy of NRM, York)

In October 1845, nearly four years after steam trains had commenced services on the London to Brighton line, trials of 'atmospheric trains' began between Forest Hill and Croydon. Had they proved successful then traction methods for many years to come could have been revolutionised. The system professed itself to be clean, fast and almost noiseless. Speeds of over 60 mph were claimed and, in a later run, 70 mph was claimed with a six vehicle train. For a time many considered that steam trains would be phased out!

In June 1827 a meeting had been held in Brighton where

support was given to an atmospheric line from London to Brighton for 'the conveyance of passengers between Brighton and the Metropolis' and an extension to Shoreham Harbour 'for the transit of goods'. A company called the 'London, Brighton and Shoreham Pneumatic Conveyance Co' was formed and annual profits were anticipated at 10%. Unfortunately for the promoters, lack of finance forced them to drop the idea.

In 1838 a similar patent granted to Samuel Clegg (previously a gas engineer) and Jacob and Joseph Samuda (shipbuilders) had led to practical results. In essence the idea was that a train would literally run on air, being a combination of a partial vacuum and atmospheric pressure. The system eliminated the need for locomotives but required the laying of a continuous iron pipe between the rails. Stationary engines by the trackside pumped the air from the pipe which had a continuous slot in it covered by a leather flap hinged on one side and able to be lifted off the other.

The leading carriage had a rod fitted underneath which carried a piston inside the pipe. Two wheels in front of the attachment lifted the flap in front of the rod and a small wheel behind sealed it again. It was the vacuum ahead of the piston and the atmospheric pressure behind it that propelled the train.

Disadvantages were many. It was expected that the vacuum would more or less cease about the time the train reached its next stopping point and a handbrake would not be necessary to bring it to a halt, but this did not always happen. Reversing was not easily possible since the piston only moved forward. Because of this trains frequently had to be moved, either manually or by a horse with a tow-rope or even on occasions by the unfortunate 3rd class passengers! Alternatively the track had to be built on an incline.

When reversing became a necessity at the end of a line it was quite a complicated business. The piston assembly had to be unbolted from the piston carriage and the latter turned around, then the piston and its driving arm refixed to the train. Further problems appeared to be that a satisfactory system of constructing points had not been worked out and also level crossings were difficult because of the pipe between the rails.

Advantages also existed, claimed the inventors. They

33

included reduced permanent way costs, no smoke or dirt, and also high speeds were possible. Elimination of collisions was a fact since only one train could be between pumping stations at any one time.

Trials began on the West London Railway in June 1840 in the Kensington area which were considered successful. In August 1840 the idea was put to the London & Croydon Railway but no immediate decision was made. Meanwhile the Irish Government granted a loan of £25,000 to the Dublin & Kingstown Railway for an experimental line to be built between Kingstown and Dalkey. This proved successful, operating over a single track nearly two miles long. Regular services commenced on 18th August 1843 lasting some twelve years.

The London & Croydon Railway's shareholders showed interest in the idea and a decision was made on 7th March 1844 that an independent atmospheric line should be built from London to Croydon. Parliamentary approval was given in August 1844.

Stage one of the construction was to be from West Croydon to the Dartmouth Arms (now Forest Hill). Stages two and three proposed a line to New Cross and London Bridge and finally stage four was planned to Sutton and Epsom from West Croydon. A separate track, to be built on the down side between Forest Hill and Norwood, was considered necessary so as not to impede the longer distance services of the London & Brighton Railway (L&BR) and the South Eastern Railway (SER). Between Norwood and West Croydon the atmospheric trains had to cross the ordinary tracks and because of this the first ever fly-over bridge in the world was built. The length was about 700 yards and it was a timber construction. The approach to the bridge was later replaced by an embankment which still remains in evidence today.

The Epsom branch was initially sponsored by an independent company although the L&CR originally had ambitious ideas that atmospheric trains would eventually reach Portsmouth! Between Croydon and Epsom plans were made for a single track with a crossing loop at Carshalton (renamed Wallington in 1868) thus allowing a regular hourly service. How the promoters would have overcome the points problem does not

An article in the October 1845 edition of 'Illustrated London News' shows an engine house for atmospheric trains. They were given 'architectural' treatment to make them less unsightly and the final result resembled more a steep-roofed church and steeple than an engine house and chimney. (Photograph courtesy of NRM, York)

appear to have been recorded. Other intermediate stations planned included Sutton, Cheam and Ewell (now Ewell East).

Pumping stations on the initial stretch were at Forest Hill, Norwood Junction and Croydon. The stations were given 'architectural' treatment to make them less unsightly and the Norwood Engine House ended up resembling more a steep-roofed church and steeple than an engine house and chimney. The 'stations' were operated by pairs of single cylinder beam engines fired by a mixture of coal and coke.

By late summer 1845 the first trial between Forest Hill and Croydon took place. Optimism was soon dashed as mechanical failures started to occur and in some cases engine crankshafts broke. Public opening was delayed. Despite the earlier successful trials, 1845 proved a disappointing year and it worsened when, in November of that year, one of the Samuda brothers, Jacob, was killed by an accident to one of his steamships on the Thames.

Troubles persisted with work on the Croydon to Epsom line suffering delays over difficulties in acquiring certain areas of land. Also the 'steeple' on the Croydon engine house had to be removed as it had become unsafe due to heavy vibration. Expenditure on the engine houses was continually increasing. Eventually a public opening was fixed for 19th January 1846, but when the day came two engines broke down and the atmospheric system had to suffer the indignity of having steam locomotives to assist. The service was withdrawn.

By Easter 1846 the weather took a hand in worsening matters with the period proving the start of a very hot summer. The flap at the top of the tube (through which the arm projected) became ineffective because the heat melted the mixture of beeswax and tallow intended to seal the area. As bad luck would have it, the winter that followed was a bitter one. Temperatures as low as minus 11 degrees Centigrade (12 degrees Farenheit) were recorded causing the leather of the valves to crack which caused further leakages.

All this required additional pumping. Further complications arose when rubbish was sucked into the pipe and then expelled to pumping stations. There are stories that even rats were drawn into the system! Air valves were choked and train workings deteriorated further. Although trains resumed publicly in July 1846, there remained instances of failure to stop at stations and of buffer collisions at Croydon when rails were greasy.

The end came nearer when in the same year the L&CR amalgamated with the L&BR to become the London, Brighton & South Coast Railway (LBSCR). The new company became increasingly disillusioned about atmospheric trains and later in the year the board asked Joseph Samuda if he would like to work the trains for a period on a contract basis. Samuda, still convinced that his idea had a future, experimented with a trial run from New Cross to Croydon, with no intermediate stops, to convince any doubters. The train, a piston carriage and three vehicles with a total weight of over 16 tons, reached Croydon in twelve and a half minutes giving an average speed from start to stop of 36 mph.

But this was not enough to win overall support and the case for abandoning the system was strengthened following a serious fire at West Croydon in September 1846 which destroyed the atmospheric shed and ten carriages. The directors decided to investigate the project's finances and by the end of the year discovered that as much as £228,290 had been invested in the New Cross to Croydon line and £186,169 in the Epsom branch.

By March 1847 the LBSCR, not surprisingly, gave up the system altogether. The atmospheric railway had lasted officially just over a year during which time a plan to extend from New Cross to London Bridge had been shelved and work already carried out on the stretch from West Croydon to Epsom had been abandoned. The steam locomotives had won their day.

The engines, atmospheric tubes and all other equipment were offered for sale but there were no buyers. Finally much of the gear was auctioned fetching minimum scrap value only. Only the engine house at Croydon North End aroused interest. On 21st May 1850, the Croydon Local Board of Health, requiring a

Originally part of an engine house used with atmospheric trains at West Croydon, the building was moved to Surrey Street, Croydon in 1851 where it became a pumping house for local main water supplies. (Author)

new pumping station for the main water supply, approached the LBSCR with an offer of £250. This was accepted and at the end of the year the building was removed to a new location in Surrey Street, where, despite many alterations and additions, it remains to this day. The Forest Hill engine house survived until 1944 when it was hit by a flying bomb.

4
The 'Overhead Electrics'

Locomotive no 198 hauls a passenger train southwards through Clapham Junction station. Wires for the 'Overhead Electrics' (1909-1929) can be clearly seen. (Lens of Sutton)

It is easy today to take the 'third rail' electric trains for granted but there was a period when working with overhead cables was used in parts of Surrey. Such a service was extended from London to Coulsdon North and to Sutton on 1st April 1925, but the system lasted only four and a half years. On Sunday, 22nd September 1929 the last AC 'Overhead Electric' train left Victoria and stock was converted to the now familiar DC traction.

As early as 1901 an idea for a monorail system was put forward for an independent electric railway from London to Brighton. The scheme was originally based on the Behr

Monorail principle similar to a project previously authorised between Liverpool and Manchester. A terminus was planned at Lupus Street in the Pimlico area of London and at Brighton a station was to be considered at the Metropole. Between Cane Hill and Redhill a 3½ mile tunnel would accommodate trains under the North Downs. There would be no stations along the route but loops of some length through important areas, such as Croydon, would be incorporated to allow through or separate trains. It was reckoned the journey would take 32 minutes at a cost of 5/- return first class!

Because a rival monorail scheme, backed by a London syndicate, was being considered and since Brighton Council were showing no interest in any such systems, the original ideas were changed considerably. Tracks would include a continuous viaduct from Waterloo to Croydon with 'a roadway for vehicular traffic underneath' and at Brighton an elevated terminus would be built at Furze Hill with passenger approach by hydraulic lifts. Intermediate stations would be sited at Croydon, Redhill, Horley and Haywards Heath. In addition the cost had escalated, from an estimated £6m to £9m, and the journey time increased to 40 minutes.

Brighton's feelings about such plans were hardening. Certain elements of Brighton's society were against the idea for fear it would encourage 'large numbers of day trippers'. When the Bill for the project, submitted by the London & Brighton Electric Railway, reached Parliament it was rejected.

The following year there was another proposal on the Behr system but this time using LBSCR property. It was rejected by the railway company's directors and the Bill was withdrawn. But the challenge remained for the LBSCR which felt some counter-action was necessary. It also felt spurred to greater effort by a report in *The Times* which had expressed dismay over the London to Brighton line, describing it as a 'crawl to the South'.

The fastest train on the LBSCR timetable was then the 5 pm from London Bridge which reached Brighton in 1 hour 5 minutes. On Sunday, 26th July 1903 a train left Victoria comprising three Pullman cars and a brake van hauled by the B4 class *Holyrood* to cover the 50 miles 73 chains in 48 minutes 41 seconds. The average speed was 63.4 mph with the maximum of

90 mph being attained near Horley. The return journey took 50 minutes 21 seconds. Thus the company considered they had not only shown the capacity of their steam trains but also demonstrated their effectiveness against the possibility of electric traction.

An 'unusual' idea was put forward in November 1905, when a concern suggested a roadway from Croydon to Patcham (north of Brighton) to carry vehicular traffic. It was to be known as a 'motor-way' but the Bill was withdrawn in February 1906. Clearly the idea was well before its time!

Despite the LBSCR's reluctance to consider electric trains, it was inevitable that they should come about. With quadrupling on sections of the Brighton line in hand, the company conceded that this would give them 'two tracks for the latest novelties in traction'. Ultimately it was falling receipts on the South London suburban lines and also increasing competition from London's trams that forced the situation, since by now the LBSCR was losing business at an alarming rate. It was eventually accepted that the only alternative to the drastic step of closing

An LBSCR southbound locomotive, no 210 'Fairbairn' class B2, hauls an express at Wandsworth under electric overhead wires, c1920. The LSWR line can be seen separating on the left of the picture. (Lens of Sutton)

41

uneconomic routes was electrification. Operating costs would be reduced and, with greater acceleration, more trains could be run.

By January 1909 electric trains were being run between Battersea Park and East Brixton. Work was carried out by Robert Blackwell and Co, with materials coming from the Allgemeine Elektricitats Gesellschaft – known as AEG of Berlin. Soon electric trains were extended to Peckham Rye, and by December 1909 a line from London Bridge to Victoria had its public opening. The trains were running on a 6,700 volt 25 Hz AC overhead wire system. Success was immediate. The trains proved, as expected, more efficient than their steam counterparts and traffic increased. They became known as the 'Elevated Electrics' but were soon referred to as just the 'Overheads'.

By 12th May 1911 similar trains reached Crystal Palace from Victoria via Balham. The line was opened in time for the Festival of Empire held at Crystal Palace and opened on that date by King George V. Work on the Tulse Hill line was completed in the same year although this section was never brought into regular

An 'Overhead Electric' train emerges from Crystal Palace tunnel. 'Overheads' reached Crystal Palace from Victoria via Balham on 12th May 1911. (Lens of Sutton)

use. Soon lines with overhead cables extended to Norwood Junction and Selhurst. These latter two were brought into use earlier than expected to economise on the use of coal for locomotives, due to a coal strike early in 1912.

The three-coach units initially employed on the suburban routes were quickly withdrawn partly because there were too many first-class compartments. When two-coach units were introduced they proved immediately popular. Future plans included electrification to East Croydon and Coulsdon North, West Croydon, Sutton and Cheam and another to Sutton via Mitcham Junction. Cheam had been included due to the inadequacy of sidings at Sutton plus the fact that Cheam was a fast growing residential suburb. The rolling stock used on these services was of a different type. Instead of power bogies being fitted under the passenger-carrying coaches, separate motor vehicles were used and a typical formation would be a five-car unit with the motor unit third. Each motor van was fitted with four 250 hp single-phase motors and often two five-car units would be run together to cater for peak traffic.

But in 1914 the war came and all progress was halted. It was

LBSCR D1 tank no 298 hauls a single coach at West Croydon under electric cables. (Lens of Sutton)

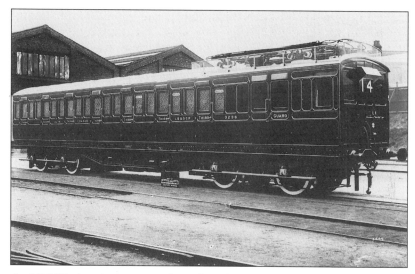

An LBSCR electric motor coach used on the South London line services. (Lens of Sutton)

Southern 'Overhead Electric' motor coach no 10114 as used in May 1927. Previously this coach had been used as a milk van. (Pamlin Prints)

particularly affected because much of the project involved the use of German equipment. Work was slow to pick up again after 1918. In 1921 plans were forwarded to electrify the Brighton line but there were no immediate results. The planned extensions to Coulsdon North and Sutton were started in 1922. Work on these lines was carried out by GEC no doubt under license from AEG, the German counterpart. Cable supports to Coulsdon North were built by 1923 but the catenaries and conductors were not finished until autumn 1924. When both services finally opened on 1st April 1925, Carshalton Beeches (formerly Beeches Halt) on the Sutton line was still being enlarged.

The 'Overheads' lasted until 1929 by which time the Southern Railway decided that any further progress would be standardised on the 'third rail' low voltage DC system already proven elsewhere in the region. In addition it had been found that costs for the overhead equipment had been higher than anticipated. The change-over on the former LBSCR lines began in June 1928 with 'third rail' services commencing between London Bridge and Coulsdon North, and by September 1929 'third rail' trains reached Sutton and Coulsdon North from

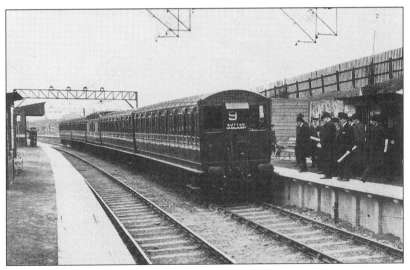

An 'Overhead Electric' train en route to Sutton at Carshalton Beeches. The service to Sutton opened officially on 1st April 1925. (Lens of Sutton)

A Billinton C2 class 0-6-0 no 542 passes under overhead electric cables at South Croydon, c1925. (Lens of Sutton)

Victoria. Such was their popularity that a new electric line was built on the third rail system from Wimbledon to Sutton (via St Helier) and opened by 1930.

At the same time the Southern Railway announced a plan to electrify the line from Coulsdon North to Brighton via Redhill and the Quarry Line together with a branch to Reigate. The total cost including new stock and resignalling was estimated at approximately £2,700,000 but it was considered this would be more than offset by an anticipated increase in annual train mileage from just under 2 million to nearly 5 million.

Work began in 1931 with many signal boxes demolished under the new signalling system and a total of 285 new coaches were provided which included 38 Pullman cars. Electric trains reached Three Bridges on 17th July 1932, and from that date, Salfords Halt, originally built in October 1915 for the employees of the nearby Monotype Works, was brought into public service. The service to the coast was formally opened on 30th December the same year. An attraction of the new service was the hourly non-stop run from Victoria to Brighton which reached its destination in just an hour. During tests a run was completed in 46 minutes 43 seconds, almost two minutes faster than the LBSCR's *Holyrood* in 1903!

Press reaction to the new trains was good. An article in *The Times* said the third class carriages were 'quite as comfortable as the first-class carriages on our most progressive lines in pre-war days'. The feature praised the trains for not belching 'stifling smoke through Merstham Tunnel' and finished with some stern advice, hardly heeded today, 'After this foretaste of electric luxury let who will creep at their own and others' peril along the highway: sensible and self-regarding persons will stick to the train.'

By 1939 many lines had been converted and a new electric branch to Chessington South from Motspur Park had been completed. Plans to electrify the Oxted line had to be shelved when the Second World War broke out but the proposal reached fruition when electric trains reached East Grinstead in October 1987.

There is no doubt that the 'Southern Electric' service has proved highly successful but it also had its critics. With the third rail operation, adverse weather can quickly throw a whole section into chaos. When the electric services began, the railway authorities advertised, 'You won't need a timetable'. Perhaps, when the conductor rail is coated with ice, they could well be right.

5
Branches Around Guildford

Guildford station in the days of steam around 1909 when tracks left the junction in six different directions. (Pamlin Prints)

When the first train steamed out of Guildford station destined for Woking at 7.30 am on 5th May 1845 there was free beer all round, despite the early hour, for the workmen who had built the line. It was an occasion of great celebration and the journey of just over six miles was completed in twelve minutes.

Guildford has been a meeting place of travellers throughout the centuries. Once an ancient market town and a centre of local agricultural life, it was also famous for its cloth making and as a stopping place for the Portsmouth coaches. It was not surprising that its importance grew when the railways arrived.

The Guildford Junction Company was authorised to build the short branch from Woking in 1844. Initially it was planned that

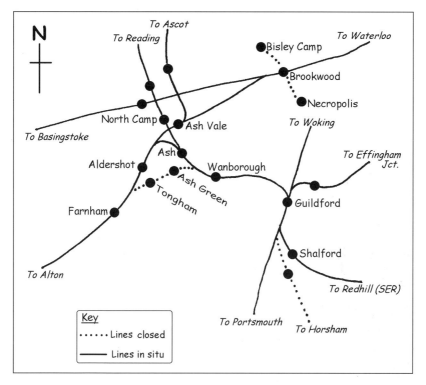

the trains would be far from conventional, to be run on what was known as Prosser's system. The idea comprised engines and coaches using flangeless wooden wheels to be run on flat wooden track with additional guide wheels pressing at angles to the sides and the tops of the rails. When Prosser had patented his idea in 1844, he claimed that his locomotive had travelled about 3,000 miles during a period of two months without any repair necessary. One of the main features demonstrated was that under such circumstances a train could not derail.

In fact any mileage completed must have been during trial runs on Wimbledon Common where a circular test track of ten chains radius had been constructed including gradients of up to 1 in 50. A further trial line existed near Vauxhall Bridge where experiments were watched by numerous engineers.

The Guildford company successfully sought the support of

the LSWR but the latter was far from happy with the Prosser system. The scheme would in any event have prevented through working of LSWR trains thus requiring an unnecessary change at Woking. Perhaps it was just as well for the future of railway history that the LSWR, when purchasing the line, insisted on conventional trains. At least for William Prosser the LSWR purchase price for the Guildford Junction Company included a sum of £2,000 compensation. But this was not quite the end of such a system. Prosser's idea, or something quite similar, was used in France in 1848 on a 25 mile line from Paris to Limours lasting over 40 years.

Further lines from Guildford were soon to follow. In 1849 a link to Farnham was established and in 1852 this was extended to become the Alton line. Both these areas were barley-growing districts and a heavy traffic of locally brewed ale was expected. Hitherto some 145,000 barrels had been conveyed annually by road to Winchfield on the main Basingstoke to Woking line for conveyance to London. Extra freight was expected from stone quarries near Alton, previously not exploited through transport difficulties.

Guildford continued to grow in importance as a railway junction. Also in 1849 an SER line from Redhill and Dorking opened to link with GWR lines at Reading, being part of an ambitious scheme to reach the Channel ports from the Midlands and the West. Initially the connection was useless since the GWR at that time operated a wider gauge but eventually an Act of July 1854 rectified this anomaly. In 1865 LBSCR trains reached Guildford from Horsham (see Chapter 13) and twenty years later trains reached Guildford from Hampton Court junction (on the main Woking line) via Cobham.

Immediately south of Guildford station, St Catherine's tunnel and Chalk tunnel are located. These were obviously negotiated with alarm in earlier times particularly since in 1876 the northern end of Chalk tunnel had collapsed. Apparently a train passing through stopped in such good time that a passenger gave over £9 for the driver, fireman and other staff to share! There was trouble too in St Catherine's tunnel when the crown collapsed in 1895. An empty train was trapped without injury to staff and an hour later was buried by another fall. It was nine

Busy steam days at the Guildford 'Roundhouse' locomotive shed in August 1953. (Pamlin Prints)

Tongham station on the original line from Guildford to Alton which closed to passengers on 4th July 1937. The station became unstaffed from December 1926. (Lens of Sutton)

51

days before single-line working was possible.

Guildford station dates from a reconstruction in the 1880s which included seven facing platforms and a short bay. It also had a coal stage, loading docks, a goods shed, stables and a corn store. To the south was the familiar 'Roundhouse' locomotive shed which survived until the demise of steam. A subsequent historic event for Guildford station was the arrival of electric trains in July 1925, an event that was loudly proclaimed by the Town Crier!

The route today from Guildford to Alton takes a traveller through Wanborough, Ash and Aldershot to Farnham but the original line took a more south westerly direction through Ash Green and Tongham. These stations were closed for passenger traffic when electrification came in July 1937 and the stretch was finally abandoned in 1961. The line was not without its incidents. In 1862 an LSWR goods train went out of control down the gradient towards Guildford station to collide with an SER goods train. The enginemen managed to jump to safety before the impact. There was another accident when, five years later, ten people were injured when an SER train was hit by another from Alton, due to a signalman's error.

At Ash Green there was an incident which set a pattern for the future. The intention was to detach a horse box and carriage from a Guildford to Southampton train so that a wagon which contained the furniture and effects of a transferred signalman could be added. As the train reversed to regain the horse box and carriage, the buffers were contacted but trouble with coupling caused the vehicles to jump the scotches (wooden structures swung across the line) allowing them to reverse down a gradient. Porters threw ballast on the line whilst the guard tried to scotch the wheels but in vain. Four passengers jumped to safety before a goods train was struck at Ash junction. As a result of the accident, rear brake vans became a necessity on all trains in future on the line.

Ash Green station building still remains today, attractively restored as a private residence. The old trackbed has become a bridleway maintained by the local authority. Tongham station not far away has been demolished. The station building which once stood astride the platforms on the overbridge has gone. A

Ash Green station closed in 1937. The station building, photographed in April 2002, has been attractively converted to a private residence. (Arthur Tayler)

Stones each weighing about 5 cwt with some bearing drilling holes. Found near the site of Tongham station, photographed by the author in July 1987. Research suggests these were used as sleepers in sidings on the Tongham line probably as early as the turn of the 19th/20th century and that they remained in use for many years. (Author)

A bridle path exists today where over 60 years ago steam traffic passed. The path has been continually improved through Council grants. (Arthur Tayler)

section of the trackbed west of Tongham has been used for the new Runfold Diversion Road, also part of the new 'Blackwater Valley Route' which diverges to the north.

During a visit by the author to Tongham in July 1987, a number of square stone blocks lying in the grass near the station site caused some excitement. No doubt found under the platform during demolition, it is thought likely they were originally stone sleepers from the sidings at Tongham station. Each block weighed about 5 cwt and some had been drilled, presumably to take the cast iron chairs necessary to secure the rails.

At its height, Guildford handled trains in six different directions. Although spacious, it was considered to be awkwardly laid out and at one time LSWR notices were displayed advising passengers not to board a train before ascertaining its direction. Perhaps some passengers today may experience the same feeling!

6
An SER Line Across Surrey: Redhill To Reading

Steam and electric stand side by side at Redhill on 19th August 1961. The locomotive is a class U1 2-6-0 no 31894. The two-car electric is a Reigate shuttle. (John H. Meredith)

The Reading, Guildford & Reigate Company was incorporated in 1846 to build a line nearly 46 miles long from Reigate (Redhill from 1849) to Reading where it would join the main GWR line to the West Country. The route was quite a complicated one running south east from Reading to Farnborough, then on to Ash junction where it joined the LSWR branch from Alton. From Ash junction through Guildford to Shalford junction, running powers over LSWR lines were agreed and from Shalford the route was back on its own metals following the southern slopes of the North Downs to Reigate.

The line took a long time to build and was considered to be poorly constructed. It had been approved by Acts of 1846 and 1847 with a further Act dated 1849 to cover the company's use of LSWR metals from Ash to Shalford junction. First lines to open were on 4th July 1849, from Reigate to Dorking and Reading to Farnborough. In the following month, trains reached Shalford from Dorking, and Guildford from Farnborough. Whilst waiting for the Shalford-Guildford stretch to open, passengers had to be content with a horse-bus connection. It was not until 15th October the same year that the line was completed throughout.

In 1852 the SER decided to buy the line, a decision which antagonised many shareholders who were unhappy about the high price offered and who had doubts about the viability of the route in general. The SER Chairman had argued that the line served as an invaluable link between the Great Western Railway (GWR) and the south east coast ports, yet rather neglecting the fact that, at that time, there was no continuation beyond Reading because of the GWR broad-gauge track. Despite the fact that a 'Regulation of Gauge Act' had been introduced in August 1846, the situation at Reading was not regularised until 1858, some twelve years later.

The line could have assumed greater importance when, in 1859, a company called the Portsmouth Railway, formed in 1853, completed a line between Guildford and Portsmouth via Godalming and Havant. A link between Godalming and Shalford was given approval which would allow Portsmouth trains to reach London via Reigate on a route 12 miles shorter than the LBSCR route to the capital via Brighton. Work started on a curve to join the two lines and a wooden trestle bridge was built over the river Wey. Even a building was constructed for an intended station at Peasmarsh. However, the SER decided to honour an agreement with the LBSCR not to 'poach' in another territory and the spur was removed before completion. Had it remained, Shalford could perhaps have become an important railway junction.

Earlier in 1854 the Government had financed the building of army camps near a small village called Aldershot, and by 1855 North and South Camps were officially opened by Queen

56

Victoria. This of course encouraged some traffic on the otherwise quiet SER line and by 1858 a station on the Reading line was opened at North Camp. The first station built was on the north side of the level crossing but several years later the present long, low station buildings were constructed on the south side where there were ample sidings. Today the station has kept its prominence, serving Gatwick-Reading stopping trains, currently Thames 'Turbo' two-car or three-car units of classes 165 and 166.

Ash station opened in August 1849, when the line began, but Wanborough opened much later, in September 1891. Between Ash and Wanborough the earthworks from the old Tongham line can still be determined. An unusual feature concerning Wanborough station was an agreement that platform tickets should never be sold!

Beyond Guildford, Shalford station had a complex goods yard plus a narrow-gauge tramway serving a timber yard. There was a small loco-shed and a large depot for making up trackwork. Truly the makings of an important junction had that spur to the Portsmouth line been built. On a recent journey by the author, the train stopped for only a few seconds at Shalford with no passengers getting on or off. Now permanently unstaffed, today's station is reduced to two short staggered platforms each with a metal shelter. What a sad decline.

After Shalford came Chilworth and Albury, now called simply Chilworth. Here the railway picks up the course of the Tilling Bourne with Chilworth being another unmanned stop. The original gabled and decorated station house is now let out for private use. In his book *Railways of the Southern Region*, Geoffrey Body writes that in the old signal box, it was not unknown for the signalman to find a snake nestling under the floorboards! And the barrier crossing is now CCTV operated with the old gates now in use on the Dart Valley Railway.

Gomshall station opened with the line and was originally called 'Gomshall and Shere Heath' until the temporary station was replaced by a permanent structure. Like other stations along the line it had a large goods siding. There was also a branch to a nearby sandpit – today used by a caravan sales company. Dorking Town (now Dorking West) and Deepdene stations have been reduced to mere 'bus-stop' type platforms.

Chilworth & Albury station (today known as Chilworth) opened on 20th August 1849. In this April 1997 photograph a Redhill bound three-car unit, no 165108, is about to depart. (Arthur Tayler)

Dorking West (formerly Dorking Town) has today been reduced to a 'bus-stop' type station. A Redhill to Guildford train awaits departure in October 1992. (Arthur Tayler)

Deepdene opened in February 1851, as 'Box Hill and Leatherhead Road' to be renamed Box Hill in the same year. In 1923 it acquired its present name.

Nearby Deepdene House (demolished 1969) achieved fame in the last war when the Southern Railway used it for its wartime headquarters. It was there that, day and night, throughout hostilities, experts planned the movement of special trains and equipment for the forces with particular emphasis on pre-D Day activities. The author writes this paragraph with some pride, for his father, Victor Oppitz, was a member of the railway staff at Deepdene and was closely involved with troop movements, yet never once breathed a word of his work.

In 1867 a single line spur was built to link the SER line between Deepdene and Betchworth with the LBSCR route from Leatherhead to Epsom. The spur never saw regular traffic and was lifted in 1926 but was relaid as a temporary measure during wartime in 1941.

Betchworth retains its original 1849 gabled-style building on

At Betchworth the former station house has survived the years. The ground floor is used commercially while upstairs has become the home of a former railwayman. In earlier times sidings led to a nearby quarry working. (Arthur Tayler)

the down side although this is now used privately. The station was once noted for its extensive railway system serving lime works to the north. There were three gauges, standard, 3 ft 2¼ ins and 1 ft 6 ins. The 3 ft 2¼ ins quarry line closed in 1959 but the locomotives 0-4-OT *Townsend Hook* and *William Finlay* (Fletcher and Jennings, 1880) were independently acquired for preservation in 1960. After various locations they were united again at Amberley Chalk Pits Museum near Arundel in West Sussex. A further locomotive, 0-4-OT standard gauge *Baxter* (Fletcher and Jennings, 1877), was delivered in 1960 to the Bluebell Railway at Sheffield Park. Today the quarry line is no more. The derelict office at the entrance was demolished at a later date when the site was taken over for use as a rubbish tip. Only a reversing siding survives from the 'up' side as a reminder of the past.

Reigate station opened as 'Reigate Town' when the line began. The original tall-chimneyed and multi-gabled buildings on the down side have gone but the up platform remains much the same. When electrification came to the Brighton line in 1932, the short section to Reigate was included whereupon many semi-fast trains to London had four coaches from Three Bridges and

A Reigate to Tonbridge train (3H 205029 in BR green) waits departure at Reigate station on 25th August 1993. (Arthur Tayler)

60

A Gatwick to Reading train about to depart from Reigate on 26th March 2002. The picture shows modern buildings following the down platform's demolition. (Arthur Tayler)

A three-car unit, 165105, leaves Redhill travelling southwards for Gatwick on 14th September 1996. The line to the left is used by trains bound for Tonbridge. (Arthur Tayler)

four from Reigate joining at Redhill's platform 2. At one time it was intended to build a spur at Redhill to give through running from Reading to Brighton and it was no doubt inter-company rivalry that ensured that this did not happen.

The Redhill to Reading section remains a vital link as a route to bypass London. Apart from Virgin trains making for the South Coast from the North, services include diesel units of two or three cars between Gatwick Airport and Reading. Plans to upgrade the Reading/Redhill/Tonbridge route to speedily access freight traffic from the Midlands to the Channel Tunnel still remain a possibility. There is even talk that a flyover might be built at Redhill to give Reading to Tonbridge trains a through run without a reversal at Redhill which at times is congested enough. Perhaps in the not too distant future the SER dream of such a direct cross country line avoiding London will at last become a reality!

7
An SER Line Across Surrey: Redhill to Tonbridge

Locomotive no 31831 class N 4PSF hauling an LCGB Maunsell Commemorative Rail Tour stands at Redhill station on 3rd January 1965. (John H. Meredith)

When Parliament sanctioned a line from London to Brighton in 1837, MPs considered, with total lack of foresight, that one rail entrance into London from the south was sufficient. Because of this the SER was obliged to accept that any major route they planned to the east should commence at Reigate (later known as Redhill) with part of the remaining route from London to be shared with the rival London and Brighton Railway. Under such circumstances a line from Reigate to Tonbridge was built eventually reaching Dover in February 1844.

The first (L&BR) station opened in July 1841at Redhill on the Brighton line known as 'Reigate', by which time L&BR trains had reached Haywards Heath. The Redhill (SER) station for trains to Tonbridge (then spelt Tunbridge) opened less than a year later in May 1842. The two 'Redhill' stations were badly sited, being at each end of Hooley Lane, then a muddy, ill-lit road. Despite frequent complaints from travellers, the inconvenience continued for two years after which time a joint station was built at the present site, where the lines separated. The name remained 'Reigate' until 1849 when the SER opened a line westwards to Dorking and the present Reigate station (then called Reigate Town) came into being. The confusion was regularised when the original Reigate became Redhill.

Redhill station was rebuilt in 1858 on the site of the earlier 1844 station with part of the original buildings remaining at the south end, down side. Redhill has been 'rebuilt' many times with the last major change taking place in 1933. Many considered the station had been a 'nightmare' to work in busier times. In earlier days during holiday periods there were

Looking northwards towards Redhill Junction, c1910, (known as Redhill since 1929) where track left the main line to Tonbridge to the east and Reading to the west. (Lens of Sutton)

constant arrivals and departures including GWR trains splitting into different portions.

In May 1868 a new SER main line from London to Tonbridge via Sevenoaks was opened which reduced the company's dependence on the Redhill route. Although fewer trains now ran via Redhill (SER) to the Kent coast, the route continued to play an important role over the years to come. In 1884 a double-track spur was built (between Godstone and Edenbridge) connecting the SER cross-country route to the newly opened Oxted line (joint LBSCR/SER owned) to allow trains from Croydon to reach Tonbridge and beyond. When the Mid-Kent line opened in 1885 linking Woodside with Selsdon, SER trains were also given a through facility. Although the spur was removed in the 1960s it had served a useful purpose, not only for SER local services but also for excursion and goods trains from London to the Kent coast.

In the years that followed the line settled to a quiet existence. Apart from its growing use for cross-country services to the rapidly expanding holiday resorts, it was perhaps not until the First World War that any changes were seen. Much of the traffic then comprised troop or hospital trains in addition to supplies being moved to the Channel ports.

After the war the railway was in a very poor financial condition and it did not really recover until after 'grouping' in 1923 when the Southern Railway was formed. This was also a time when the route served a new purpose. From 1920 the Redhill-Tonbridge line was followed by pilots of the new air service from London to Paris since the navigational aids of the day were not sufficiently reliable. To assist pilots the names of Redhill and Tonbridge were painted in large letters on the station roofs to guide the planes back to the airport.

No doubt the line saw 'its finest hour' at the time of Dunkirk from 27th May to 4th June 1940. During that period there were no less than 565 special trains from the various ports all running to Redhill with many on to Reading. All regular services were stopped for the period and troop trains ran as and when they were required.

After the war, with the return of petrol, many passengers were lost to road traffic. Instead a commuter service to London gradually built up with many travellers coming from Nutfield and Godstone. Also due to the then inadequacy of the nearby Oxted line, many more were coming from Edenbridge in Kent where there was a choice of station and route. With the end of steam now in sight, the future of the line became uncertain although somehow it managed to escape the Beeching axe. Thoughts of possible future military use or the prospect of a Channel Tunnel secured the line's future. In 1969 there were plans to electrify many lines including the Tonbridge-Redhill route. BR claimed in 1987 that plans were still in hand but 'due to continually changing circumstances no commitment could yet be given'. Today, 15 years later, such plans are no further forward.

Nutfield opened in 1883 and was in a modern style compared with earlier stations. Sidings existed including a long one to a chemical works put in almost 60 years ago where tank wagons were worked by Southern Railway locomotives.

Between Nutfield and Godstone lies the 1,326 yard Bletchingley tunnel. During the Second World War there was a Home

Nutfield station photographed on 6th March 1997. The four-car unit 1565 is the 11.43 am train from Victoria to Tunbridge Wells. Nutfield station opened in 1883. (Arthur Tayler)

Guard post at the eastern end and it is said that on occasions drivers of goods trains would slow down and, on seeing a board held up bearing the word 'Coal', they would drop off a few lumps to keep the Home Guard's brazier going!

At Godstone the platforms were built slightly staggered probably due to a nearby embankment. The station was opened with the line in May 1842, but in 1914 it acquired a new building on the down side. Standing some three miles south of Godstone village, it was no doubt responsible for the smaller village that sprang up around it called South Godstone. Today the station's sidings have gone and the buildings have been replaced by unattractive shelters.

In the early days of the SER, whistle signals from locomotives were also used to inform pointsmen or signalmen of a train's direction. At Redhill, non-stop down trains whistled once if bound for Tonbridge, twice for Brighton and three times for Reading. How the staff in the Computer Room at the Three Bridges Signalling Centre would shudder at such a thought today!

8
Brookwood – A Cemetery And An Army Camp

A funeral train passes Wimbledon on 25th June 1902. The train had two 'religious' portions each with its own hearse van. (Pamlin Prints)

The Brookwood Necropolis Railway

The Brookwood Necropolis Railway, a short branch line off the LSWR main line between Woking and Farnborough, served an extensive cemetery and was certainly one of the more unusual branch lines. There were two stations on the ¾ mile single-track line and it seemed that the final destination (in the earthly sense) depended upon one's faith since the North station was built for Nonconformists and Roman Catholics and the South station for Anglicans!

It was probably the cholera epidemic of 1848/9 which had caused nearly 15,000 deaths in London alone that brought about this vast cemetery of nearly 2,200 acres in the Surrey countryside. The London Necropolis Company (LNC) was incorporated in 1852 and the scheme established in 1854 after numerous delays. In London a private terminus was built off York Street, near Waterloo.

In June 1863 the LSWR acceded to requests from local inhabitants and the LNC for a new station on the main line to be provided near the cemetery. Hitherto the nearest main line stop had been at Woking nearly 4 miles away. When Brookwood (Necropolis) opened on 1st June 1864, the land had been provided by the LNC which also built the approach roads and the station-master's house.

Initially the railway company did well, gaining not only from the journey to the cemetery but also from subsequent visits by relatives. The trains consisted of normal coaches for the mourners and special hearse vans for the coffins. Charges for the conveyance of corpses were apparently high.

On arrival at Brookwood, the train was backed into a siding parallel to the down local line, after which it was propelled to the cemetery under the guard's supervision. The journey to North station was only a quarter of a mile and the terminus at South station was half a mile further on. In each instance the brick-faced platforms were lowered halfway along their length to facilitate the unloading of coffins.

Brookwood station was enlarged in 1890 but when main line quadrupling was carried out from Woking to Basingstoke during 1898/1902, the down platform was demolished to make way for the new tracks. A new platform was built on the cemetery side and there were extensions to buildings on the up platform.

Meantime in London, the site of the original York Street station was needed by the LSWR for necessary widening of tracks into Waterloo and by an agreement dated May 1899, the LSWR accepted the cost to construct a new Necropolis station and offices. The new terminus, a tall four-storey building housing the LNC offices, opened in February 1902 and was situated at 121 Westminster Bridge Road, just south of Waterloo station. Entrance into the station was through an impressive archway.

The Necropolis branch line came to a sudden end on the night of 16th April 1941, when high explosive bombs fell on the Westminster Bridge Road station sidings. Not only was the Necropolis train damaged but also much of the station and buildings. Nothing could be done to restore the service until after the end of the war when, soon after May 1947, the LNC offices were transferred to Brookwood. The decision not to restore the Necropolis train service at that time seemed logical since the motor-hearse had now taken its place.

By 1953 the branch line track had been removed and in the 1960s the North station was demolished. South station continued as a refreshment room until 1967. After closure it became a store but on 22nd September 1972 half the building was destroyed by fire apparently caused by vandals. When the remainder of the building was demolished later, a chapter in history had come to an end, and since that time only the outlines of the two platforms have remained as a recollection of the past.

The branch line from Brookwood to Necropolis closed in 1941. The track had been removed by 1953. Necropolis North station was demolished in the 1960s because of dry rot. (Lens of Sutton)

The remains of Necropolis North station photographed in July 1987. (Author)

Necropolis South station which closed in 1967 after having served for a time as a refreshment room. After closure it became a store until it was burnt down in 1972. (Lens of Sutton)

71

The Bisley Camp Branch

The Bisley Camp branch line to the west of Brookwood opened in 1890 and closed in 1952. The object of the short line, about 1¼ miles long, was to link the Bisley Camp of the National Rifle Association (NRA) to the main Waterloo-West of England main line. During the First World War, however, the branch was extended westwards to connect the military camps formed at Pirbright, Deepcut and Blackdown.

The original site for the NRA ranges was at Wimbledon Common. In 1864 a tramway was built to convey competitors and spectators from a camp on the common to the ranges. It was a straightforward layout with no points or sidings and the track gauge was 2 ft. Six four-wheeled wagons were provided for passengers which were drawn by military horses running alongside the track rather than between the rails. As can be expected, the tramway proved quite an attraction and it is understood the fares were 2d return and 1d single. In 1877 a steam tramcar was made available to the NRA comprising a

Push-pull set no 721 with class M7 0-4-4T no 128 at Bisley Camp station, c1947. (Lens of Sutton)

boxed-in design and weighing about 4 tons. The locomotive, capable of pulling six fully-loaded wagons, was inaugurated by the Prince of Wales. It was named *Wharncliffe* and was to play a role in later years at Bisley.

When the NRA was given notice to leave Wimbledon Common in 1888, a new site at Bisley was adopted on an area of government land. Two years later, by 12th July 1890, the short branch line from Brookwood to Bisley Camp had been completed. The first train, hauled by an LSWR Adams 02 class 0-4-4 no 185, conveyed the then Prince and Princess of Wales along the line with the engine especially named *Alexandra* (after the Princess of Wales) for the Royal occasion. At Bisley huge crowds welcomed the Royal guests and the new Bisley line was declared officially open.

When moving from Wimbledon, the NRA had transferred the small tramway to Bisley. By 1898 this had been installed to carry competitors and spectators the mile journey from Bisley Camp station to the ranges. Also transferred was the tram engine *Wharncliffe* and its set of wagons. Soon afterwards a further 2 ft

Two-coach motor unit 734 stands at Bisley Camp station on 18th July 1952. Trains on this branch line had sometimes been referred to as the 'Bisley Bullet' or the 'Bisley Flyer'. (John H. Meredith)

gauge tramway was added to transport targets to the range butts. Although some tracks were later removed, the line to the 'Century' butts survived to be worked by a Lister 2-cylinder diesel engine.

When the First World War broke out, the NRA placed its facilities at the disposal of the War Office. Soon Bisley Camp was occupied by regular soldiers and during the first four months of the war some 150,000 men had undergone training at the site. By 1916 the camps in the area had become quite extensive and it was agreed that an extension from Bisley should be built to include Pirbright, Deepcut and Blackdown to be served by a line about 3 miles long. This was completed by March 1917, with an opening ceremony performed by King George V and Queen Mary whilst visiting soldiers in the area. In 1919, after the war, the NRA resumed its normal meetings and the 3 mile extension was probably lifted during the early 1920s.

In 1939, at the outset of the Second World War, Bisley again assumed importance as a centre for small arms training and research. Two years later the branch was extended once again but this time only for about one mile to reach the outskirts of

'Wharncliffe', the Merryweather tram engine, at Bisley Camp, c1907. (Lens of Sutton)

Pirbright Camp. After the war, however, the branch and extension were not to survive many years. The Pirbright extension was probably lifted by 1950 and the Brookwood to Bisley Camp line closed in early 1952 after over 60 years of faithful service. To mark the closure, the Railway Correspondence and Travel Society organised a special journey in November of the same year using an LSWR push-pull set of two coaches borrowed from the Clapham Junction to Kensington service (previously used on the Plymouth-Turnchapel service) and hauled by M7 class 0-4-4T no 30027.

The majority of the track was lifted by November 1953, although a spur remained as a siding for many years. This was later removed. At Bisley Camp station the platform is still there and in 1984 the building became the home of the Lloyds Bank Rifle Club. As a reminder of its railway days, the Lloyds club obtained a former Mk 1 BR Sleeping Car which was erected on a short stretch of specially laid track to provide extra sleeping accommodation for club members.

Other reminders of the past can easily be found with platform edges and bridge abutments in evidence. Deepcut Camp

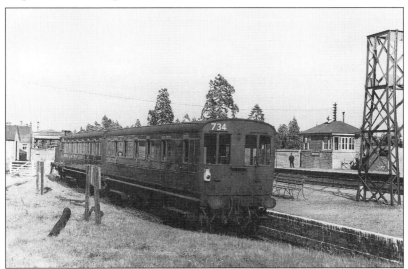

Bisley Camp branch motor unit 734 photographed at Brookwood on 18th July 1952. The branch closed in the same year. (John H. Meredith)

station, which survived many years as a Royal Army Ordnance Corps (RAOC) Museum, had a concrete-faced platform but the building was wooden. The walls were made from logs by Canadian troops when the line was first opened in 1917. But even this has now gone since the museum acquired a new home in 1970 and eventually the station building was demolished.

9
Battles Along The Caterham Valley

A locomotive and three coaches arrive at Purley, celebrating the Caterham branch's centenary 1856-1956. Note the top hat by the driving cab. (John H. Meredith)

Mention 'Halliloo Platform' to any commuters on the comparatively busy Caterham Valley branch line today and they will probably never have heard of it! It was a little-frequented halt consisting of just one platform in place from 1897 to 1900 during a period of reconstruction and improvement. Used mostly by parties of school-children, it was removed when Whyteleafe station opened on 1st January 1900.

When the London & Brighton Railway opened its main line in 1841, the nearest stations to Caterham were at Godstone Road

77

(now Purley) and at Stoats Nest (near Coulsdon). A year later the SER opened a line from Redhill (then Reigate) to Tonbridge (then Tunbridge) giving a station at Godstone. Within a few years there was local interest for a line to reach Caterham, although with the village having a population of less than 500 in 1851, the plans were more to reach the local quarries with their fine output of good quality firestone. At that time there was much demand for furnaces, chimneys and hearths and much potential lay beneath the chalk of the North Downs.

The Caterham Railway Company was incorporated although its ideas for lines or possibly tramways to reach quarries near Godstone Hill and War Coppice were not agreed. An Act finally received Royal Approval on 16th June 1854 agreeing the branch as it is known today. The company was an independent one but its activities immediately interested the LBSCR and the SER which were soon to become bitterly involved in battles over the line.

In his book *The Caterham Railway* (Oakwood Press) Jeoffry Spence writes that the single-line track was declared ready for traffic on 21st September 1855 but both the LBSCR and the SER

Caterham station in the days of steam. Public services began on the Caterham branch on 4th August 1856 after bitter inter-company squabbles. (Lens of Sutton)

were unwilling to allow the other to work or lease the line, so a series of delays postponed the opening. Finally the Caterham company managed to persuade the LBSCR to let them have 'an engine and two or three carriages' to make an opening of the line possible. The service was inaugurated on 4th August 1856 and public traffic began the next day.

There were two intermediate stations, at Kenley (named Coulsdon until December 1856) and Whyteleafe South (Warlingham until 1956). Godstone Road station (now Purley) was described as 'a single platform with a rough shed for passengers'. The original LBSCR station at the site had closed on 30th September 1847 having been partly dismantled with the platform shelter going to Bexhill station in Sussex.

The LBSCR had refused to reopen its station for, it was claimed, 'reasons of public safety'. They considered the Caterham Railway to be SER sponsored but when services from Caterham commenced the LBSCR grudgingly gave way. Even then it had not been until a few days beforehand that the LBSCR had agreed to stop their trains to give connections to London and the coast. At this stage, the name of Godstone Road station was changed to Caterham Junction although for a time the

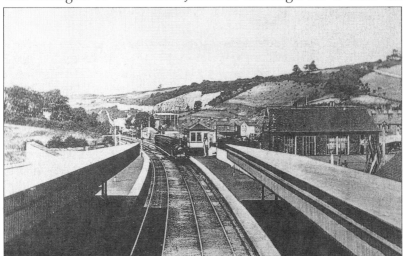

A tank locomotive and passenger set approaches Whyteleafe during SECR days, c1906. (Lens of Sutton)

Caterham Railway continued to use the old name. Initially there were four trains each way daily with three on Sundays.

From the start the Caterham line did not pay. The railway company tried hard to find passengers by offering season tickets to London at £7 a year first class and £5 a year second class to people building houses on the company's property. Further trouble between the LBSCR and the SER ensued. Because of the earlier delaying tactics, the Caterham company sued the LBSCR. In retaliation, the LBSCR caused trouble over the hire of rolling stock. Meanwhile the LBSCR had been doing its best to acquire the Caterham line, offering less than half its original cost, a move which seriously antagonised the SER. The last hope that the Caterham company might survive was lost when a contractor claimed he was still owed a considerable sum of money and, if not paid, he would pull up the rails. In November 1858 the Caterham Railway Company applied for powers to sell or lease the line to the SER. On 21st July 1859 the SER acquired the Caterham Railway for £15,200 – it had cost almost £40,000!

However, the battle between the giants was by no means over. Following disputes elsewhere over territory, relations worsened and in 1862 the LBSCR forbade the use of East Croydon station to the SER insisting that all passengers arriving from the Caterham branch should hold LBSCR tickets. In further aggra-vation, the LBSCR then timed trains to leave Caterham Junction before branch passengers could possibly rebook. Worse was still to come when passengers were forcibly prevented from boarding SER trains at Caterham Junction. Finally it was the floods of complaints published in *The Times,* then at the height of its power, which compelled the LBSCR to give way.

In 1875 an interesting scheme was put forward by the Metropolitan & Brighton Railway. Proceeding southwards from Beckenham, tracks would have passed close to Warlingham village to cross the Woldingham Valley Road by viaduct. After negotiating a tunnel under Tillingdown, trains would have reached Caterham close to the present station. Further south trains would cross to East Grinstead before travelling via Lindfield to Brighton. The idea of course came to nothing and Caterham did not get its direct link with the coast.

On 1st October 1888 Caterham Junction was renamed Purley.

According to records it acquired its name from the Pirelea family who once owned the district with one ancestor, Reginald de Pine, dating back to 1332. The change had followed pressure from the Post Office which was complaining that mail for Caterham Junction was finishing up in Caterham.

At the end of 1899 work began to double the track and improve the service. This was completed by 1st January 1900, by which time Caterham station had been rebuilt and the old station demolished. At the same time a new station opened at Whyteleafe. Inevitably competition was to come from motorbuses. In the booklet *Caterham and Warlingham – Jubilee History* (The Bourne Society), Jeoffry Spence tells an amusing account as to how in 1907 Caterham got its first (unofficial) vehicles. Apparently buses used earlier in Hastings had failed because of competition from electric trams. After the fleet had been laid up over the winter of 1906/7, trouble was anticipated because of certain unpaid accounts so in April 1907 all the buses set out for London. Many of them failed to travel more than a few miles but two, still able to climb hills, got away. One

Whyteleafe station photographed early 1980s. Whyteleafe opened on 1st January 1900. Previously passengers had been served by Warlingham station (Whyteleafe South from 1956). (J.F. Bradshaw)

Caterham station, 20th June 1964, when it had a goods and coal yard. (John H. Meredith)

BR 2-6-0 locomotive no 78038 standard class 2 returns light from Caterham on 5th July 1964 after working the LCGB 'The Surrey Wanderer' Rail Tour. Note the connection in foreground from the down Caterham platform to the down Redhill – long since gone! (John H. Meredith)

eventually reached Tonbridge before giving up the ghost and the other expired at the top of River Hill, Sevenoaks. Both were brought on to Caterham where one was repaired with parts from the other. The two drivers then ran this bus providing a service between Caterham and Godstone, covering a route where previously plans for trains had failed to establish themselves. Eventually the bus was withdrawn since it was not adequately licensed and a regular service did not commence until 1914.

The Caterham Valley line settled over the ensuing years to build up useful commuter traffic. On 25th March 1928 'third rail' electric trains reached Caterham, some of the earliest such trains to be used in the Central section. It was not until January 1933 that electric services reached Brighton, Hove and Worthing. Services improved on the Caterham line and building develop-ment was evident everywhere along the valley.

There are only a few reminders of the old days along the line – perhaps the best example is the attractive high-gabled station house at Kenley. Yet part of the old ancestry is still evident. Trains for the Caterham branch still emanate from Charing Cross, reflecting the times when Charing Cross was an SER station.

The high-gabled station house at Kenley, c1910. The station opened originally as 'Coulsdon' in 1856. (Lens of Sutton)

10
From Epsom To Horsham
Via Box Hill

The LBSCR station at Epsom (later Epsom Town) which closed to passengers in March 1929. (Lens of Sutton)

Epsom's first railway station was situated near the east end of the High Street. Earlier it had been expected that atmospheric trains from the London & Croydon Railway would reach the town but, due to their lack of success (see Chapter 3), it was finally LBSCR steam trains that arrived from West Croydon on 10th May 1847.

The Epsom & Leatherhead Railway company, formed in 1856, opened on 1st February 1859 as a joint LBSCR/LSWR venture. On 4th April 1859 the LSWR completed a line from Wimbledon to Epsom and because of this Epsom had now acquired two railway stations – the new LSWR station on the present site and the LBSCR Epsom (later Epsom Town) station near the High Street (closed to passengers in 1929). The first service to Leatherhead on the opening day was provided by the LSWR on 1st February 1859, with LBSCR trains following on 8th August of the same year when a link between the two Epsom stations had been built. Initially the line to Leatherhead was single and an LSWR timetable of 1860 informed intending passengers that 'an extra five minutes should be taken on each journey' whilst the line was newly-built! Rivalry between the companies remained. When the LSWR had built its station at the junction of the lines at Epsom, the track layout had been designed in such a way that LBSCR trains were located on through centre tracks and thus prevented from calling at the platforms.

The Leatherhead to Dorking line began services on 11th March 1867; at about the same time the line from Epsom to Leatherhead was doubled, giving double track throughout. By 1st May the same year, trains had reached Horsham, connecting with the existing 1848 line from Three Bridges and also the route from Horsham to the coast which had been completed four years earlier. In 1885 the LSWR reached Effingham Junction from its Leatherhead station to connect with the New Guildford line from Surbiton to Guildford which had opened in the same year.

The situation with rival stations virtually side by side at Leatherhead lasted until 1927 when post-grouping rationalisation took over. The Southern Railway altered the layout by providing a new bridge over Station Road for the Effingham Junction line with the result that the former LSWR station could be closed.

Today the old LBSCR station, a listed building, remains with its fine herringbone brickwork pattern and ornamental tower. On the down side the numerous arches cannot fail to impress and the decaying chimney has been restored with matching bricks. For many years the old LSWR track remained parallel to the 'new' through track for use as carriage sidings but today this has been lifted and the area built over. Nothing remained of the original 1859 station except an old engine shed that continued in use until 1874. Afterwards the shed was leased out as a church

Leatherhead station, formerly LBSCR and today a listed building, photographed on 23rd March 1988. The station opened in March 1867. (John H. Meredith)

and school at £15 a year and in 1986 it was in use as an engineering works.

Journeying southwards through the 530 yard long Mickleham tunnel and crossing the river Mole, the station of Boxhill and Westhumble is reached. Popular with walkers throughout the years, the station, opened with the line in 1867, was attractively built to match its surroundings thanks to the stipulations of the original landowner. The main complex is on the down side with the station building steeply gabled in the French style and with decorative tiles and an ornate tower. Originally opened as West Humble, the station has had many name changes, acquiring its present title after four variations!

Not far from the station, just off the A24, visiting travellers can find a public house called the Stepping Stones. This is named after the well-known stones of the same name which cross the nearby river Mole providing the start of one of the pedestrian routes to Box Hill's summit. The sight from the top will not disappoint those who struggle up its steep paths. On a clear day

Boxhill & Westhumble station, opened as West Humble on 11th March 1867, remains popular with walkers. A lengthened London Bridge to Dorking unit 4SUB is about to depart. (Lens of Sutton)

there is a splendid view overlooking Dorking and the many villages beyond. The viewpoint itself is a large memorial recalling the memory of Sir Leopold Salomons of Norbury Park who first gave land in the area to the National Trust.

It is considered that Box Hill acquired its name (it was previously called White Hill) when box trees were planted there during the reign of Charles I by the Earl of Arundel. Apparently the trees grew abundantly with stems of nearly 9 inches in diameter and the wood was highly prized for its close fine grain and its beautiful golden colour, which made it suitable for products such as chessmen, parts of musical instruments and decorative inlay for fine furniture. By the early 19th century the box trees had gone and only bushes remained.

Between Box Hill and Dorking the line on its west side borders Denbies, the largest vineyard in England. The area is dominated by an extensive winery in the French style. It is perhaps appropriate that Denbies wines were chosen to celebrate the opening of the Channel Tunnel.

Some of Dorking station's earlier buildings have survived the years on the down island platform but on the up side the station facilities have been combined in a commercial development. Electrification came to the Epsom-Leatherhead-Dorking route on 12th July 1925, at the same time as the former LSWR link from Leatherhead to Effingham Junction. Both were considered speculative ventures since many of the areas were still rural, but they proved very successful. At Dorking alone, the sale of season tickets more than quadrupled in only eight years.

Less than two months after trains had arrived at Dorking, a new line opened to Horsham with services commencing on 1st May 1867. At the same time a spur was opened linking the LBSCR line with the SER east-west line although this was little used (see Chapter 6). Intermediate stations were Holmwood, Ockley (for a time known as 'Ockley and Capel') and Warnham (in Sussex). The whole route from Leatherhead to Horsham was in fact promoted by an independent concern – the Horsham, Dorking & Leatherhead company – but, in 1864, a year after its approval to proceed, it had amalgamated with the LBSCR.

Unit 3403 awaits departure at Horsham station. The line between Dorking and Horsham is double track throughout and sometimes proves useful as a diversion from the main line through Three Bridges. (Anthony Rispoli)

Holmwood station, unlike many on the route, was built on a bridge across the track. In its time it has enjoyed quite an extensive goods yard with gunpowder vans often seen in the sidings bringing materials for the nearby Schermuly Pistol Rocket Works where the 'Verey Light' signal flares were made. The goods yard closed in 1964 although the goods shed had been demolished earlier, in 1958, since it had become unsafe. Surprisingly a solitary up siding was electrified in 1938 and for many years a London stopping service terminated there every hour using the siding when not required. The siding was lengthened in 1961 to accommodate new rolling stock but fell from use in 1975.

Ockley, like its neighbour, also once had numerous sidings. Dating back to the 19th century, an extensive 11 acre brickyard, at Jayes Park, stood close by and up to three wagons of bricks a week left the area. The works closed in 1914 but bricks were railed out again from 1938 from the nearby Phorpres Works. There was an Army Command Supply Depot at nearby Okewood Hill during the last war which gave additional heavy traffic.

In the book *Southern Main Lines Epsom to Horsham*, Vic Mitchell and Keith Smith write of a substantial 'memorial bush' on the down side about two miles south of Ockley. According to local hearsay, it was planted and tended in memory of a ganger who was struck by a locomotive whilst walking to the Northwood up distant for fog signalling duty. At Northwood a signal box was erected in 1899 to meet increasing traffic. It had only four levers in use and was manned just at peak times until it ceased to be used after 1956. Apparently when the machine room window was broken, it was never repaired since this would have disturbed the nesting routine of some local house martins!

A recollection of Christmas 1930 when special rates were offered for the holiday period. (Lens of Sutton)

11
A Day At Croydon Races –
Addiscombe And Woodside

A passenger train hauled by a Terrier locomotive emerges from Woodside tunnel between Bingham Road and Coombe Road stations on the Woodside to Selsdon branch. (J.F. Bradshaw)

Trains first reached Croydon (Addiscombe Road) along an SER branch line from New Beckenham (on a New Cross to Beckenham Junction line) in 1864. Initially Elmers End was the only intermediate station.

It was the nearby Croydon Racecourse that brought about the opening of another intermediate station – at Woodside, which opened in 1871. Horses were often brought to the racecourse by train and, for a number of years, a track to the course from the down side of Woodside station catered for many of the famous

*Woodside station, which opened in 1871, served a nearby racecourse.
Picture c1910. (Lens of Sutton)*

horses of the time. To this day, a doorway with a high arch exists
close to the ticket barrier, constructed so that horses could reach
the adjacent Ashburton Park without climbing to the road level.

The racecourse had been established at Stroud Green around
1862 and was located opposite Ashburton Park, now the site of
Ashburton High School. A number of race meetings were held
each year with an important steeple-chase event in March from
which many fine horses were engaged for the United Kingdom
Grand Handicap. This Croydon meeting occupied a high posi-
tion in the steeple-chasing world, equivalent to that of Epsom in
flat racing. Aintree was still a lesser rival.

The racecourse at Woodside was important enough to attract
many well-known people of the time including the Duke of
Hamilton, Lord Beresford and Mr Richard Marsh (the Royal
trainer). During Queen Victoria's Golden Jubilee in 1887, 10,500
school children were invited to join in celebrations held on the
racecourse. The area was at the height of its popularity.

However, the railway which had encouraged the number of
visitors was now becoming its downfall. Crowds increased and

there was insufficient supervision. It was claimed that too many undesirable people were coming to the area and efforts were getting under way to bring about closure of the track. By the end of 1890 the local movement for the abolition of Croydon Races was successful and the local licensing authority refused to grant a regular renewal. The last meetings took place on 25th and 26th November 1890, and a quiet locality many miles to the south called Gatwick was inaugurated as a successor.

Until the Second World War the area became the home of Beckenham Golf Club. Subsequently it was a site for the Woodside Fire Station and the stables in Lower Addiscombe Road were used as winter quarters for a circus. The stables gave way to a housing estate and where the entrance to the saddling paddock and grandstand from Shirley Road once stood, Shirley Park Road can now be found.

Earlier, in 1878, the LBSCR and SER reached an agreement on the construction of a line from Croydon to Oxted (and beyond) and Section 18 of the Act specified that the two companies were

At Woodside station a high arch still exists adjacent to the former down platform where once horses left for the nearby Croydon Racecourse which closed in November 1890. (Author)

to share ownership. With the SER line reaching Addiscombe, it was expected that the company would want access to the new (shared) Oxted line. This would also provide it with an alternative route from London via Lewisham and New Beckenham thus avoiding the LBSCR stations of New Cross (later New Cross Gate), East and South Croydon.

In August 1880 the independent Woodside and South Croydon company received approval to go ahead. It planned to build a route leaving the Addiscombe branch at a point immediately south of Woodside station to link with the Oxted line south of South Croydon just after the latter had left the main Brighton line. In 1882 the independent company was acquired by the LBSCR and SER jointly.

Considerable earthworks and numerous bridges were necessary to complete the line. Three short tunnels were built quite close together to be known as Woodside, Park Hill and Coombe Lane. In all some eight bridges were necessary and it was not until 10th August 1885 that services could begin. At the fork where the Oxted line was joined, a station was built called Selsdon Road (later Selsdon and now closed). Initially the only intermediate station

An SECR railcar in the Selsdon branch bay at Woodside, c1906. (J.F. Bradshaw)

Addiscombe station building from the road, photographed in the early 1980s. The whole area has today given way to a housing estate. (J.F. Bradshaw)

The wooden signal box with its semaphore signalling at Addiscombe station, early 1980s. In the siding stands a weed-killer train used on the Woodside to Selsdon branch. Beyond are the carriage sheds which were said to be haunted! (J.F. Bradshaw)

The former Woodside station building is today boarded up. The station once served trains from Elmers End to Addiscombe and also to Sanderstead. The high-arched exits for horses can be seen on either side. (Anthony Rispoli)

Selsdon station in the early 1980s. On the right the electrified branch to Woodside and on the left the line is about to join the main London to Brighton line at South Croydon. A track off to the left leads to an oil siding. (J.F. Bradshaw)

was Coombe Lane (later Coombe Road) but two stations were to follow in 1906, being Bingham Road and Spencer Road Halt.

During the First World War, the intermediate stations closed. In March 1915 Bingham Road and Spencer Road Halt closed, and in January 1917 Coombe Road followed suit. Spencer Road Halt, located off Croham Road not far from the present South Croydon station, never reopened but Bingham Road and Coombe Road came into use again in September 1935, when the line was electrified. Even so, Bingham Road was relegated to becoming a halt. Electric services ran stopping trains between Charing Cross and Sanderstead using the Woodside-Selsdon line and became known as the 'Sanderstead Electrics'. It was never heavily used except for local commuting.

The Addiscombe line was electrified in 1926 when the terminus was renamed 'Addiscombe'. Carriage sidings were built and sheds were constructed to store and clean rolling stock. According to writer W. B. Herbert in his book *Railway Ghosts*, the sheds were haunted! Apparently at night, when stock was berthed, the vehicles were isolated from the third rail and the hand brakes screwed down tightly for safety reasons. But on more than one occasion, the brake compressors were

An SECR railcar approaches Coombe Road (opened as Coombe Lane in 1885), c1906. (Lens of Sutton)

A Croydon tram passes Coombe Lane in snow. Not far away was Coombe Road railway station on the Woodside to Selsdon branch which closed in 1983. (Stephen Parascandolo)

heard running even though disconnected. Each time the shunter had to again 'cut out' the train. In addition carriage doors were heard to open and close and, perhaps strangest of all, trains were heard to move in the shed.

It seems that many years ago a shunter was killed between two units while coupling a train and some think he 'returned' to carry out these frequent manifestations, On one occasion a shunter witnessed an apparition when waiting outside the sheds. He saw a figure in grey coming out of the building walking towards him and was very frightened. But the features were blurred and then suddenly the figure disappeared. The truth of these stories was of course doubted by some but, it still has to be said, there certainly have been many strange happenings at the site in years past.

Nearly seventy years later in 1994 the carriage sheds were closed since they were considered unsafe. An adjacent wooden signal box burnt down in 1996 which involved trains using only the down line and requiring a pilotman to work with the train.

Why the signal box burnt down remains a mystery. Perhaps it was a coincidence the box was due to have a preservation order put on it. The line from Elmers End to Addiscombe via Woodside closed two years later on 31st May 1997. After closure of Addiscombe station a group was set up with the intention of preserving the station and turning it into a museum. Application was made to get the station building listed but the council decided to demolish it in June 2001, just weeks before the order was likely to be served! Woodside station building is still there although boarded up. The trackbed is now used by Croydon Tramlink on its route from Elmers End to Croydon and on to Wimbledon.

Croydon Racecourse is very much a thing of the past, having closed well over a century ago. It is doubtful if many of the local residents of today even know it had ever existed.

12
Trains To Epsom Racecourse

An LBSCR Stroudley D1 0-4-2T approaches Sutton from Epsom Downs in 1883. (Lens of Sutton)

The first ideas of reaching Epsom Racecourse by rail came in 1838 when the railway authorities arranged for trains on the newly opened London & Southampton Railway to be stopped near the present Surbiton station – then called Kingston. Eight trains were planned on race days and passengers were set down at a point where the Kingston to Epsom road crossed the line, after which a 6 mile journey on foot or by cart or trap was necessary.

The service began on Derby Day but many were disappointed. Over 5,000 people besieged the then London terminus at Nine Elms and, although several trains got away, the crowd eventually invaded the station and the police had to be called to restore order. Another route came four years later, also well patronised, when the London & Brighton Railway made similar arrangements for trains to take racegoers to Stoats Nest (between Coulsdon and Purley) after which a walk or ride of over 7 miles was necessary.

Racegoing on Epsom Downs has long had its place in history. Pepys' diary of 1660 tells of 'horse racing that took place daily at noon, and cudgel-playing, wrestling, hawking and foot racing in the afternoon'. First records of horse races go back to about the time of James I's reign (1603-1625). It was not until 1844 that a railway to reach Epsom was first considered. An independent company, the South Western & Epsom Junction Railway, planned a line with the prospect of selling or letting it to the LSWR. The idea came to nothing although a similar scheme was to come later.

In 1847 the LBSCR – previously the London & Brighton Railway – reached Epsom from West Croydon and 12 years later, in 1859, the LSWR reached Epsom from Raynes Park. Race

Semaphore signals and a misty day at Sutton station in the early 1980s. Sutton opened on 10th May 1847 when a line opened between West Croydon and Epsom Town. (J.F. Bradshaw)

traffic continued to increase and it was clear a station was needed much nearer to the course itself. There was much rivalry between the companies but it was the LBSCR that eventually won the day when it took over a concern called the Banstead & Epsom Downs Railway Company which had been formed to build such a branch, leaving the existing line at Sutton.

During construction, an attempt had been made to build a terminus only 200 yards or so from the Grandstand. Such efforts were frustrated by strong opposition from the Epsom Grandstand Association which was supported by John Briscoe MP, Lord of the Manor and Freeholder of Epsom Downs. Eventually the problem was resolved by John Briscoe who sold the plot on which the present Epsom Downs station stands, over half a mile away from the course.

First trains from Sutton to Epsom Downs ran on 22nd May 1865 – just in time for the Derby. Results exceeded expectations and, on Derby Day alone, some 70,000 people travelled by the new railway. The line was double track from the beginning to accommodate the traffic expected. The vast terminus boasted

An electric service arrives at Sutton from Epsom Downs. The branch to the racecourse opened on 22nd May 1865 – just in time for the Derby! (J.F. Bradshaw)

nine platforms with 'middle sidings' to house additional trains or to be used for 'engine release'. The platforms were not covered and the only roofed area was part of the terminal building behind the buffer stops. There was a 42 ft turntable and a tank house with water columns which were placed at the end of four platforms and a siding.

The station-master at Epsom Downs must have been a busy man at times for, in addition to his normal duties, he also ran a nearby amusement park – with company approval of course. On occasions other than race-days, the only traffic of note was the comings and goings of students to a nearby college and also numerous school parties or Sunday school outings. For the latter two, station signs even included 'Boys' and 'Girls'!

Prior to the new line, Sutton had been a small two-platform station but, when the Epsom Downs branch began, new waiting rooms and booking offices were built. These were situated mainly in the fork of the old lines and the new tracks, the latter curving away sharply to the south from the double-track junction to the east of the station. The first station to be reached was called California, known today as Belmont.

How it acquired its original name relates to a local resident charged with poaching. At the time the punishment was transportation but the victim did not fancy this idea so he escaped to America to eventually join the Californian gold rush from which he became quite rich. When he returned to this country he built a public house and called it the California Arms and it was from this that the local station took its name. Troubles soon followed since goods destined for the area were frequently exported to California, USA! So the poor station-master, burdened with complaints for lost consignments and fearing for his health, asked that the station should be renamed Belmont. The LBSCR agreed and it was changed in 1875.

The California Arms became the California and it is now known as Belmonts Restaurant and Country Carvery. The present building was erected in 1955 since, during the last war, the pub suffered serious bomb damage in April 1941 when ten people were killed and many injured. It was here that Private Gibb distinguished himself when, for three hours, he held up loose debris while buried women were rescued. For his

Banstead station 1984. The station has changed little over the years but the double track has been singled. (Lens of Sutton)

Derby Day 1907 at Epsom Downs station. On the extreme left the Royal Train with 4-4-2 tank locomotive no 600 at the head. (Lens of Sutton)

outstanding efforts he was awarded the BEM and a plaque on the wall of Belmonts commemorates the event.

At California station there was initially a goods yard between a level crossing and the Brighton Road bridge. The area was very restricted and a wagon turntable was necessary but, when the level crossing was replaced in 1888 by the present steeply humped bridge, the sidings were moved to the east of Brighton Road. Before entering Banstead station, the line enters a steep cutting in the downs. The chalk excavated was dumped on either side of the track and this has now of course become overgrown. Yet these 'lumps' can still be remembered by some as 'the chalk hills'.

In 1898 Banstead station was renamed Banstead and Burgh Heath, only to be called Banstead again in August 1928. Also in 1928 DC third rail electrification was completed to Epsom Downs to include six platforms at the terminus. At the same time the down platforms at Belmont and Banstead were extended to take eight-car trains. From an annual number of passengers using the branch in 1927 at just under 330,000, the number rose by 1935 to more than 850,000.

Decline of the branch, as with many, began some 50 years ago. Cars were taking the place of trains and services were cut. From June 1961 there was a cut-back on early and late services and just over a year later most off-peak trains from London Bridge terminated at Sutton. In 1972 five platforms were abandoned at Epsom Downs and nine years later single line working was introduced using the up line. Users of the line today must indeed be anxious about the branch's future.

Gone are the thousands of racegoers of the past who arrived often in Pullman car 'Race Specials'. Gone too are the Derby Days when trains thundered through a crowded Sutton station, often double-headed, to tackle the 1 in 60 gradient up to Banstead. Surely watching the races on TV today cannot give quite the same excitement!

13
The Horsham And Guildford Direct Railway

A class D1 tank locomotive pulls pre-bogied type coaches at Rudgwick station on the Christ's Hospital to Guildford line, c1890. (Lens of Sutton)

It was around 60 years ago when Christmas shoppers and commuters alike were shot at and bombed by a German aircraft on the Horsham to Guildford branch line near Bramley and Wonersh station. The plane, a Dornier 217, first machine-gunned the Guildford-bound train and then released a bomb which exploded in the railway bank as the train was passing. The date was 16th December 1942.

Speaking to the author in 1987, Mrs Ruth Bailey of Godalming vividly remembered the incident. On the day in question she sat

A damaged passenger train, at Bramley, which was bombed during the Second World War over 60 years ago. (Branch Lines to Horsham – Middleton Press)

with her back to the front of the train which comprised just two carriages pushed by a small 'Puffing Billy'. She recalled, 'The plane attacked from the front and I heard the bullets hit, saw the plane as it flew over very low and felt the bomb explode almost instantaneously. The train halted just as it approached the first gardens in Bramley.' Her impression was that help arrived incredibly quickly, including a number of Canadian soldiers one of whom took her to hospital in a jeep.

'Battles' along the line began much earlier, dating back to 1860 when the Horsham & Guildford Direct Railway Company was first incorporated. There had been a strong body of opinion favouring an alternative route southwards from Cranleigh through Alfold to join the Pulborough/Littlehampton line, 1½ miles south of Adversane. The Horsham route prevailed but already there was division between the LSWR and the LBSCR, both wanting to take over ownership of the independent company. Further problems developed over construction and at one stage a contractor went bankrupt causing a £30,000 loss.

Finally in 1864 the LBSCR succeeded in taking over the line even though at that stage it was incomplete.

As soon as the line opened on 2nd October 1865, there was trouble at Rudgwick station. Following an inspection of the track, it had been decreed that trains could not stop there since the gradient on which it was built was too steep at 1 in 80. It was another month before the station could be opened and then only after it was completely rebuilt and a new bridge constructed over the river Arun.

Initially the service on the new line was good. There were eight trains daily with evening trains from Guildford to Cranleigh. Another service provided late trains from Horsham to Cranleigh twice weekly. However, the local press were less optimistic about its future. The *West Sussex Gazette* of 10th October 1865 commented, 'the line was likely to prove a more picturesque than profitable part of the system of the London Brighton & South Coast Railway Company'.

Before 1867 Cranleigh was spelt 'Cranley'. The change to the present spelling was made at the request of the Post Office to

Slinfold consisted of a single station building with a well-built station house attached. There was no passing loop but, until the closure of freight traffic in 1962, a signal box acted as a ground frame for the sidings. (Lens of Sutton)

Cranleigh station (which opened as Cranley) closed in 1965. Its spelling was changed in 1867 to avoid confusion with Crawley in Sussex. (Lens of Sutton)

avoid confusion with Crawley in Sussex on badly-written envelopes and parcels. Cranleigh as a village has numerous claims to fame. Opposite the parish church of St Nicholas, the hospital, founded in 1859 by local surgeon Mr A. Napper, was the first 'cottage hospital' of its kind in the country. Today it has been considerably extended but the original 16th century house is still there. The church too is interesting. The pillar bases have a 'claw' decoration and the carved head below the south transept is that of a cat. Local residents believe it gave Lewis Carroll the inspiration for his Cheshire Cat in *Alice in Wonderland*.

Unfortunately the Cranleigh line (as it became known) did not become as popular as hoped and fares rose only 18 months after the opening. Even so the line continued quietly through the years with some useful passenger and freight traffic. Much of the commuter traffic came from Cranleigh and there was freight from private sidings, especially at Baynards. In later years the platform at Baynards became renowned for its display of dahlias but unfortunately there were few passengers there to see it.

109

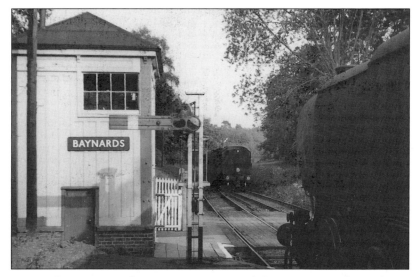

Locomotives 41327 and 33034 pass at Baynards in May 1963. The station was named after nearby Baynards Park. It had a goods station and a siding to a Fuller's Earth plant. (Lens of Sutton)

In 1896 the Light Railway Act was passed which meant that many Board of Trade requirements could be waived under certain circumstances. Under this Act, plans were deposited in the same year for a light railway to run from Ockley, on the Dorking-Horsham line, to Selham, on the Pulborough to Midhurst line, with connections to be made at Cranleigh. Nothing transpired but in 1898/9 another scheme was launched for a railway to connect Cranleigh with Holmwood, south of Dorking. Again nothing happened but had either of these taken effect, then Cranleigh could have indeed become quite a sizeable and important junction.

During the First World War the line proved its usefulness as a through route by transporting soldiers and equipment from the Midlands via Guildford to the ports of Newhaven and Littlehampton. Otherwise little changed with services continuing normally until 1917 when Sunday services were withdrawn as a wartime economy measure.

There was quite an occasion for Cranleigh School in 1935 when the Schools class 4-4-0 express locomotive of the same name visited the village to be placed on exhibition at the station. This class of locomotive had been introduced in the 1930s. Cranleigh School had been founded for the education of farmers' sons and was recognised as a public school in 1898.

At one stage in the late 1930s there was talk of electrifying the line from Guildford to Cranleigh, providing a continuation of the Waterloo via Cobham service. Existing electric services to Guildford had a 30 minute wait before returning to Waterloo and the idea seemed feasible but nothing happened and when the Second World War came, any ideas were completely shelved.

Following the outbreak of war, the line once again assumed an important role. Its usefulness as a through route was proved with the movement of troops and munitions. Baynards became a centre for military supplies and special trains used the station because a munitions dump had been set up in the park. There were frequent air attacks along the line but only one serious incident occurred as related at the beginning of this chapter. Nevertheless signal boxes in the area remained open 24 hours a day so that signalmen could report damage to any part of the line during the night.

It was probably the 1955 railway strike that began the decline of the branch. All services ceased during the period and freight traffic suffered badly, never to return to its previous level. The line was now losing money. At the same time the railways were not helping themselves. Trains were leaving Horsham a few minutes before possible connections yet there was a 15 minute wait at Cranleigh. The line had outlived its usefulness and when closure proposals were announced in 1963, they came as no surprise.

An enquiry was held at Cranleigh Village Hall but protests against the closure were minimal. With such a poor service so little used, there was no hope. The last train left Guildford on 14th June 1965 at 6.55 pm and returned at 8.34 pm. Boys from Christ's Hospital School sang *Abide with Me* as the train pulled out.

The 'Midhurst Belle Special' organised by RCTS/LCGB hauled by USA 0-6-0 tank locomotive no 30064 stops briefly at Baynards on 18th October 1964. This locomotive went to the Bluebell Railway in 1971. (Lens of Sutton)

Baynards station, now privately owned, closed in 1965. It has been tastefully restored by its present owners with the platform, buildings and goods shed appearing much as before. (Picture courtesy of Fraser Clayton)

There are numerous recollections of the line today. The site of the former Bramley and Wonersh station is now occupied by several small businesses, but its station nameplate can still be seen and a section of the down platform survives as part of the 'Downs Link' footpath. Cranleigh station has completely disappeared; its site is an open area known as Stockland Square. Goods sidings once existed in the area between today's Somerfield store and the National Westminster Bank. The station platforms were situated along the car park to the rear of the shops. Baynards station, tastefully restored, is now privately owned and no entry is allowed. The goods shed is still there and the platforms are very much as they were before the station closed in 1965. But for the absence of track, one could be convinced that the railway had not gone. In 2001 the whole station had a repaint, retaining its LBSCR colours. Commented the owner, 'And it took 16 gallons of paint to do it!'

14
Rivals Share The Oxted Line

Tank locomotive no 42074 arrives at Selsdon (opened as Selsdon Road) and waits clearance to join the main London to Brighton line. In the background the rear of the Selsdon station on the line to Woodside. (Lens of Sutton)

In the 1865 session of Parliament, a Bill was presented by the independent Surrey & Sussex Junction Railway (S&SJR) for a new line from Croydon to Tunbridge Wells via Oxted to be worked by the LBSCR. This immediately incensed the SER which claimed that it was in breach of an 1864 agreement that neither should violate the other's territory.

The S&SJR's Bill was passed on 6th July 1865 but construction proved difficult. To the north of Oxted, a 2,261 yard tunnel had to be bored in addition to two shorter ones along the line. Few bridges were required but a brick viaduct north of Woldingham was necessary. Land deals were found to be 'irregular' and there was bad rioting at Edenbridge because of large numbers of navvies imported from Belgium. Despite the railway companies' financial problems, the LBSCR/SER 'territorial dispute' continued and eventually the Duke of Richmond was asked to arbitrate. This resulted in the S&SJR being passed to the LBSCR which was immediately anxious to abandon the project. Calculating that it would cost them up to £2 million to complete the line, the company, still short of cash, decided it was easier to pay a £50 per day penalty clause with a maximum limit of £32,250.

Nothing positive happened until 1878 when the Croydon, Oxted & East Grinstead Railway (CO&EGR) obtained approval to construct a line. In the same year there was agreement between the rivals LBSCR and SER that they should share the new CO&EGR line from South Croydon to Crowhurst junction north (where a loop would join with the existing SER Redhill-Tonbridge line). From the loop southwards to East Grinstead it would be totally LBSCR owned.

As soon as work on the line started, there were delays. Under pressure from landowners and prospective users, navvies were imported to speed up the work. But, as had happened previously, there was trouble. A local newspaper of May 1882 stated, 'Lingfield Navvies assault Police: Scripture Reader puts in good plea for defence'. Apparently the navvies' disturbing presence in the area had been felt for some time but during the same period a chaplain had attended them at their 'Lingfield huts'. A chapel was used at Dormansland and some navvies received baptism. However, despite good influences, trouble appears to have persisted – and on both sides of the law. Eventually, in October 1882, application was made for two particular special constables to be removed.

The line opened on 10th March 1884, and within a few years there was access to many additional routes. These included the SER Mid-Kent line when the Selsdon and Woodside line opened in August 1885, and to Tunbridge Wells via Edenbridge and Groombridge (opened October 1888). Although the Oxted line never really acquired 'main line' status, it served for most of its life as a useful commuter and through passenger service.

A train awaits departure at Oxted station. When the line opened on 10th March 1884 it was jointly owned by the LBSCR and SER. (Anthony Rispoli)

Edenbridge Town on the Oxted line to Tunbridge Wells photographed in the early 1980s. Edenbridge enjoys two railway stations – the second is to the north of the town on the SER line from Redhill to Tonbridge. (J.F. Bradshaw)

Initial weekday services comprised four trains run by each company with the SER trains terminating at Oxted. By August, two of these used the loop at Crowhurst to reach Edenbridge and one to reach Tunbridge Junction (now Tonbridge). In 1885 the LBSCR ran four trains to East Grinstead plus three terminating at Oxted. When the Groombridge line opened in 1888, LBSCR trains reached Tunbridge Wells by a shorter route using their own Edenbridge (now Edenbridge Town) station.

The first station on the Oxted line after leaving South Croydon was Selsdon. Opened as Selsdon Road in 1885, the station was built at the point where a new line from Woodside joined the Oxted line in the same year. However, after spasmodic use through the years, Selsdon finally closed in June 1959.

As well as being a busy station on the Oxted line, Sanderstead also served for many years as a terminus for trains from London via New Cross and Elmers End using the Woodside to Selsdon

The 3.52 pm train from Victoria to Brighton via the Oxted line hauled by 'Atlantic' class locomotive no 32426 'St Alban's Head' arrives at East Croydon station in August 1953. The semaphore signals on the large gantry to the left of the picture were replaced by the following year with colour light signals. (Arthur Tayler)

link. This link closed in May 1983. In addition there had been plans around 1927 for a narrow-gauge electric railway to be built from Sanderstead to Orpington, to be called the Southern Heights Light Railway, but the project never came to anything.

Riddlesdown station, in a deep cutting leading to an 837 yard tunnel, opened in June 1927. This was as a result of local building development, supported by the newly-formed Southern Railway. Upper Warlingham opened with the line in 1884 but was known as 'Upper Warlingham and Whyteleafe' from 1894 to 1900. Once boasting numerous sidings, many were out of use by 1945 and others were gone by 1963.

Woldingham opened as 'Marden Park' but changed to its present name ten years after the line began. The nearby Marden Park acquired notoriety in the 1970s when the Government announced plans that the area might be considered as a terminus for the Channel Tunnel. Apparently the public outcry was such that the idea was abandoned.

Oxted has changed little since its opening although the platforms were lengthened at the up end in the 1960s. Like

Passengers wait at Hurst Green station (previously Hurst Green Halt) on the Oxted line. To the south lines separated for East Grinstead or Uckfield. (J.F. Bradshaw)

118

others on the line, most of its sidings have gone although a bay remains at the down end. For many years it served as a place where the East Grinstead and Uckfield off-peak services combined or separated on their way to or from London Bridge.

After Hurst Green, opened as a wooden-built halt in 1907 and resited to become the present brick structure in 1961, comes the point where the East Grinstead and Uckfield lines separate. Keeping on the East Grinstead route, Crowhurst junction is soon reached, where a spur to the original SER line diverged to the left. Now completely removed, it once served trains to Tonbridge and beyond, being particularly useful on the several occasions when the tunnel at Sevenoaks was under repair.

Lingfield seems to have been not only famous for its racecourse but also its bananas! After the Second World War, traffic developed with the construction of a ripening shed for bananas off one of the sidings at the up end. A daily train of refrigerated vans, sometimes as many as twenty, became a frequent sight. Earlier in July 1898, authority had been given for a continuation of a siding to the racecourse itself but this was

Dormans, with the station building unusually at right angles to the track, photographed around 1910. The white post is the down starting signal in the cutting. (Lens of Sutton)

119

Champagne is used to celebrate the first electric train to reach East Grinstead at the launch of services on the South East Network on 30th September 1987. This service will at a future date connect with Bluebell Railway trains when work between Kingscote and East Grinstead is completed. (Author)

never built. However, a large extra footbridge was built at the down end leading to a covered way on the course. It was this footbridge which was later removed and reinstated at Sheffield Park for use as part of the Bluebell Railway.

Dormans station, a mile or so to the south, has retained its elegant building, unusually built at right angles to the track. It has survived well over a century with its round-headed windows and ornate chimneys. Gone, however, are the covered-ways to the platforms where only a shelter exists on the up side.

When electrification reached East Grinstead in October 1987, the line increased in importance. It is well known that plans are at present in hand for the privately owned Bluebell Railway to reach East Grinstead, thus providing a station of its own adjacent to the present station. In this way the Oxted line will surely acquire a new lease of life when stations along the route will see special Bluebell excursions travelling directly through to Sheffield Park from London.

121

15
Early Days At Gatwick

Gatwick airport station in its more casual days! This is the first airport station, opened as Tinsley Green in September 1935. (Lens of Sutton)

Gatwick Racecourse station on the main London to Brighton line opened in 1891. Previous race meetings had been held in the Croydon area. There had been a racecourse at Stroud Green, near Woodside (see Chapter 11) but this had attracted so much traffic by road and rail that eventually an improved site 'in a quieter location' was chosen at Gatwick. In addition Croydon Racecourse had become the scene of much rowdy behaviour from undesirable visitors with the result it closed in November 1890, whilst the Gatwick was under construction.

To cater for the anticipated traffic, an up relief line was opened from Gatwick Racecourse to Horley in October 1892.

A general view of Gatwick Racecourse and grandstand in the early 1920s. In the foreground, the auctioneer's stand – the grandstand beyond is now in Queen's Square, Crawley. (Author's Collection)

The Parade at the old Gatwick Racecourse in the late 1920s. (Author's Collection)

This line made it possible for Gatwick station to be considerably altered under the powers of an Act agreed in 1899. At the same time a fourth line was added being an extension of the quadrupling being carried out from Earlswood to Horley.

The racecourse owners paid £5,000 to the railway authorities towards the construction of the station, which soon became an important part of the racecourse itself. The station initially served the course only, with frequent excursions on race-days. Three long covered walkways were constructed to the grandstand.

Not far from the grandstand stood a fine bandstand, obviously a centre of much entertainment in the heyday of racing. This bandstand remains intact today but at its new site in the centre of Queen's Square in Crawley. It was purchased by the local council for a mere £60.

The racecourse achieved much fame throughout its life. During the First World War, the Grand National was transferred from Aintree to Gatwick for the years 1916 to 1918. By 1930 the valuable Grand National Trial was introduced, attracting many famous horses. Special Pullman excursion trains were run on race-days and Gatwick was a popular place indeed!

Around the same time new sounds were being heard overhead with aircraft, including an Avro 504 and a Gipsy Moth, taking to the air. The son of a builder in Redhill, called Waters, had started a flying club quite near the paddock. Flying, of course, expanded and soon the racing authorities were claiming that those wishing to enjoy a day at Gatwick could now arrive by road, rail or air.

This was not the first time the railways and aircraft had worked together. Since the First World War the railway lines had always proved a reliable, and often the only, navigational aid. Pilots, often lost, would follow the Brighton line northwards as they looked for aerodromes to the south of London.

Soon farmland between the racecourse and nearby Lowfield Heath was bought to develop an aerodrome to be named Gatwick after the course itself. By September 1935 Tinsley Green railway station opened near where the original Beehive control tower still stands. The station was renamed Gatwick Airport on 1st June 1936. Racing continued until the early 1940s by which time the land had been taken over by the Government. With the country at war, priorities perhaps became confused when a final day of training on Spitfires had to be cancelled through a race meeting!

Before leaving the earlier Tinsley Green station it is worth recalling an account from J.H. Bentley's book, *Copthorne: People and Places.* Much has been heard in the past of 'The Great Train Robbers' but probably lesser known is the time when nearby Copthorne had its own 'train robbers' who were active in the area. The events go back to the 1930s when goods trains were frequently parked in a siding overnight. Not far away was the Radford Road railway bridge and it was here that certain 'adventurous groups' made frequent visits.

Stories have it that the practice was to lower a rope over the bridge parapet to where fellow conspirators were waiting below on the line and then 'goodies' were hauled up such as bacon, sacks of sugar and similar items which had been stacked in the railway wagons. When completed, the 'robbers' would carry off their loads, entering Copthorne by a little used route. Apparently all went well until one night the police were waiting in a wood for the culprits. Arrests were made and the adventures of the 'Copthorne Train Robbers' came to an abrupt end.

A down express speeds through Gatwick Racecourse station in LBSCR days. The station became the present Gatwick Airport station on 27th May 1958. (Lens of Sutton)

125

Express trains await departure from Gatwick Airport, 2002. Gatwick Expresses run very frequent services to London Victoria, the journey scheduled to take approximately 30 minutes. (Anthony Rispoli)

Gatwick Racecourse station closed in 1935. The new Airport station opened on 27th May 1958, the day before the old Airport station (near the Beehive) finally closed. The Beehive still survives of course and it has a 'ghost' as a reminder. A number of years ago, workers thought they saw a colleague walking towards them in a long, dark coat and trilby hat. But as he reached them he vanished, accompanied by a sudden and chilling drop in temperature. The old days are not forgotten.

From such modest beginnings at Gatwick, it is surely some achievement that today's trains from the airport cater for many thousands of passengers daily. The Gatwick Express started services on 14th May 1984, running non-stop from Gatwick to London. Current rolling stock is usually class 460 eight-coach EMUs with white/grey livery, red roofs and Gatwick Express branding.

Today there is only one positive reminder of the past. The old concrete passenger bridge that once spanned the early Gatwick Airport station now crosses the track at Balcombe station in Sussex, 7 miles to the south.

16
Trains Reach Tattenham Corner

Tattenham Corner station in busier times! Steam Pullman specials arrived earlier with race-day crowds, c1922. (Lens of Sutton)

A journey on the Tattenham Corner branch today shows only too sadly how decline has long since set in. Along the line many station buildings are shuttered, waiting rooms have closed and canopies have been removed. Tattenham Corner's once proud six platforms were reduced to three as early as November 1970, at a time when most of the sidings had already disappeared. All this a far cry from the days when each station had its own station-master plus porters and signalmen.

First moves for a branch up the Chipstead Valley came in the late 1860s. The LCDR had a plan to build a railway south from

East Croydon, using running powers over LBSCR lines as far as Stoats Nest (later Coulsdon North) and then curving up the valley towards Tadworth. From there the line would curve towards Banstead where tracks would fork left and right to either Epsom Downs or Sutton. No doubt through lack of finance and also lack of enthusiasm from the LBSCR, which claimed it to be their 'territory', the idea foundered.

In the book *The Tattenham Corner Branch*, N. Owen writes that the branch probably owes its existence initially to pressure from farmers in the 1880s who were becoming increasingly dissatisfied with the difficulties of cartage to farms throughout the area. Goods facilities were available at Banstead on the LBSCR Epsom Downs line but it was a fair distance from Banstead's yard to reach such places as Tadworth or Kingswood. The idea received support from wealthy residents in the Kingswood Warren area. The scheme was master-minded by an MP called Cosmo Bonsor, a Director of the Bank of England. It was soon appreciated that a railway serving the district would increase the value of the land and prices would inflate very much to the landowners' advantage. Bonsor and his friends first proposed a spur from the Epsom Downs branch to reach a point near the present Tadworth station. It would be known as the Epsom Downs Extension Railway for which capital of £65,000 was required, the majority having been already offered by Bonsor himself.

Opposition came from a local landowner who claimed his land would be cut in two. The Epsom Grandstand Association also complained. They said that the line would cross a new 'straight mile' they were proposing and horses would be adversely affected. The idea was never taken up but it did pave the way for the more practical scheme which was to follow. The Chipstead Valley Railway was formed with a cost estimated at £250,000 for a line from Purley to Tadworth. Another company, the Epsom Downs Extension Company, would cover the track to the terminus at Tattenham Corner.

A single line from Purley to 'Kingswood and Burgh Heath' opened on 2nd November 1897, although records indicate that trains actually started a week later. The only intermediate station was 'Chipstead and Banstead Downs'. Purley had been

Purley, which opened as Godstone Road in 1841, photographed probably in the 1920s. Caterham and Tattenham Corner trains used the platforms on the right. (Lens of Sutton)

rebuilt as a six-platform station partly because quadrupling towards Redhill was in hand (see Chapter 17) and also to accommodate separately the branch line trains. In January 1899, the SER and LCDR amalgamated to become known as the SECR. Bonsor became the Chairman of the SECR Managing Committee.

In the same year rivalry between the SECR and the LBSCR was further aggravated when the SECR considered building a link from the Oxted line near Sanderstead (jointly SECR/LBSCR owned) through a 580 yard tunnel under the Downs to join the Caterham and Tattenham Corner lines south of Purley at a new SECR Purley station! History shows that the idea failed.

Trains reached 'Tadworth and Walton-on-the-Hill' on 1st July 1900 and four months later the branch was doubled. Between Tadworth and 'Kingswood and Burgh Heath' were two short tunnels, built because of local objections to open cuttings through common land. One tunnel was called 'Kingswood' and the other acquired the delightful name of 'Hoppity'!

It was of course appropriate that Tattenham Corner station

should open on Derby Day, 4th June 1901. On that occasion it was recorded that the terminus handled between 14,000 and 15,000 passengers. Many came from the London stations but large numbers arrived in special excursions from the coast or through Reading. The passengers were delighted. Here was a new railway service which took its punters right to the racecourse itself. In addition to this a raised lawn close to the station gave excellent views over much of the Downs.

Three years after the line's opening, a station opened at Smitham close to Coulsdon North station (then Stoats Nest) on the Brighton line. Despite apparent duplication of services, the site could be considered important historically since not far away the line crossed the route of the Croydon, Merstham & Godstone Iron Railway, which had opened just under one hundred years previously (see Chapter 1).

On race-days, services to Tattenham Corner were in great demand but efforts to encourage ordinary passenger traffic to the terminus were less successful. Reedham Halt, close to Old Lodge Lane, Purley, opened in 1911 to encourage local traffic. The halt took its name from the orphanage at the top of the

Smitham station on the Tattenham Corner branch in the late 1980s. The station opened on 1st January 1904. (J.F. Bradshaw)

nearby hill. Three years later, in 1914, Tattenham Corner station closed for regular traffic and trains terminated at Tadworth.

Army camps were set up on Epsom Downs during the First World War and the branch saw only military trains. Tattenham Corner was used for munitions work and after the war the station had a strange role when surplus military engines returned from France to be auctioned off.

The 1920s proved an important era for the branch. On Derby Day 1923, around 40,000 people passed through Tattenham Corner station. Among the additional trains running there were many Pullman specials. In addition in the 1920s, the Royal Train switched from Epsom Downs to Tattenham Corner to become a regular Derby Day visitor.

Third rail electric trains came to the Tattenham Corner branch on 25th March 1928. Tattenham Corner station was reopened to normal services and the platforms at Reedham Halt, Chipstead and Kingswood were lengthened to take the new nine-car trains. Woodmansterne station opened in July 1932 and four years later Reedham Halt was upgraded to become known as Reedham.

There is no record of any major dislocation of services during the Second World War. However, shortly afterwards, on 24th October 1947, there was a serious accident when a Tattenham Corner train carrying about 1,000 passengers crashed in thick fog into the back of a Haywards Heath train near South Croydon station. The mishap, caused by signalman's error, cost 32 lives and many injured. The author recalls the event only too clearly. His sister Muriel was travelling on the Tattenham Corner train but fortunately she was not in a forward compartment and escaped injury.

Despite the improved prosperity following electrification, a decline set in from the late 1950s when services were generally cut back. By the early 1960s most of the sidings had gone and most off-peak trains were reduced to two cars. Many trains worked as shuttle services to and from Purley. Soon booking offices were opened at peak times only with fares collected aboard trains at other times. There was a respite in decline when, following passengers' protests, some through services were restored from May 1970, to Croydon and London.

Kingswood & Burgh Heath station on the branch line to Tattenham Corner photographed in 1987. In the early 1920s the canopy was used as an open-air tea terrace! (Author)

Tattenham Corner station, 19th January 2002. Long since gone are the days of race traffic and trippers to the Downs. (Anthony Rispoli)

Finally a recollection from the halcyon days of the early 1920s. It was not surprising that with Cosmo Bonsor resident at Kingswood Warren, Kingswood and Burgh Heath station should be a most elegant affair. The station house was three-storey and above the platform was a canopy also used as an open-air tea terrace. Unfortunately the novelty quickly wore off since tea and cakes to the accompaniment of soot and steam were obviously not to everybody's taste!

17
The Brighton Line –
Quadrupling And The
Quarry Line

The popular 'Brighton Belle' began as the 'Southern Belle', a new train of first class only Pullman cars, to be renamed the 'Brighton Belle' in 1934. (Pamlin Prints)

The L&BR received Parliamentary approval to build a line from Norwood to Brighton on 15th July 1837, the stretch from Norwood to Reigate (now Redhill) to be in agreement with the SER. The line took three years to complete. At times over 6,000 men and 960 horses were being used, many of the men being navvies from Ireland. Numerous routes had been suggested and it was finally one proposed by Sir John Rennie that was adopted.

The digging of the cuttings and embankments proved

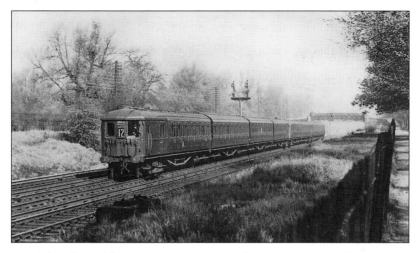

A Brighton bound four-car unit, 2944, semi-fast Victoria to Brighton, passes Wandsworth Common on 18th April 1952. (Pamlin Prints)

arduous. Barrows were filled and then hauled by horses one by one up plank walks to the top. The navvies had no living quarters and each had to make a rough shelter of turf and brushwood for protection. These were continually rebuilt as work progressed along the line. Fighting was prevalent, especially on paydays when much drink was consumed. There were strike threats when no beer could be purchased near the site and boys were often paid ½d a journey to bring in supplies.

When Merstham tunnel was dug, it was found to be riddled with disused mining galleries. In March 1840, one of these was struck by workmen, releasing a flood of water which swept away wooden supports. Part of the works collapsed and a worker was killed. When the tunnel was completed, trains could reach as far as Haywards Heath. The first train left Brighton on 21st September 1841 at 6.45 am to arrive at London Bridge one hour 45 minutes later. A special train carrying the directors and their friends left at 8.45 am. There were fourteen coaches pulled by two engines. To start with trains were first class only, to deter trippers, but there were usually two second class compartments in the front coach for servants.

A critic of the day wrote that 'the train got into a rapid motion

135

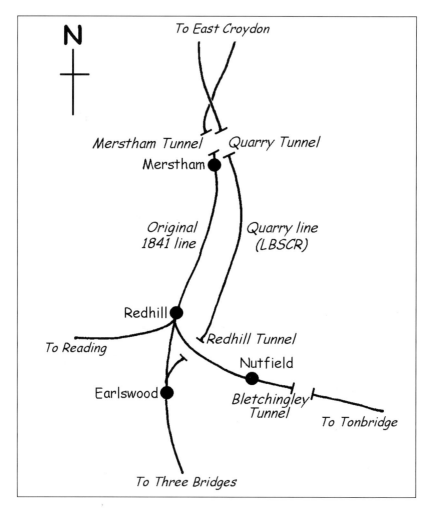

and whizzed through the cuttings and over the embankments, both of considerable magnitude'. Others said that passengers who were hurtled through the air at speeds up to 30 mph would suffer epilepsy, hysteria and many other ailments. They said that railway staff could expect to spend time in hospital due to the strain of their dreadful working conditions.

When third class travel was introduced it was frequently in open trucks without seats. By 1845 an Act of Parliament compelled the railway companies to provide coaches which were covered. Before this happened a jeweller made his name by selling special railway spectacles as protection against the dirt and steam!

When the SER opened lines eastwards in 1842 and westwards in 1849 from the station now known as Redhill, traffic on the line from Croydon southwards increased considerably. This section had been built by the L&BR but an Act of Parliament dated 1839 had stipulated that part of the stretch should be sold to the SER. Bitter rows followed and use of the line by the Brighton (L&BR) company required special payments to the rival company.

It was not until July 1845 that an SER offer of £340,000 was accepted by the L&BR board. But this did not include the purchase of a gasworks already built to illuminate Merstham tunnel and the SER directors refused to take possession of it. The L&BR was now not interested in lighting the tunnel so eventually the gasworks was sold to Lewes station where, at the time, exorbitant amounts were being paid to a local gas company to light the station.

Tunnel lighting had been a feature of the Brighton line both during its construction and when it was opened. Gas lamps had been fitted to the walls of Merstham tunnel which had also been whitewashed so that the new passengers could feel comforted in the dark. But the idea did not work for long because as the train passed through, the smoke blackened walls and the draught caused by the coaches blew out the lamps!

In February 1869 an agreement was signed whereby the payments to the SER would be based on the L&BR's (now LBSCR) gross receipts and a figure of £14,000 a year was accepted. It was a 10 year agreement and when renewal was considered in 1879, there was further trouble. The SER complained that it could not improve its services covering the new routes because there were too many LBSCR trains. In addition the LBSCR was unhappy because its trains were not allowed to stop at Merstham, the only intermediate SER station between Coulsdon and Redhill.

Finally, after continued arguments between the companies, Henry (later Sir Henry) Oakley, General Manager of the Great Northern Railway, was asked to arbitrate. This he did in July

1889 with the result that the LBSCR's payments to the SER were increased to £20,000 a year.

Meanwhile in 1888, quadrupling from South Croydon to Coulsdon (later Coulsdon South) had been considered by the LBSCR directors in order to provide independent tracks for their trains. In 1890 the company received a resolution from the Brighton Council urging the widening of the line as far as Redhill. Two years later an estimate to double the line from Croydon to Redhill was put at £370,000. Plans were prepared and a Bill was deposited in November 1893. There was of course very little opposition from the SER which could only benefit from the project and its only complaint was that the new LBSCR line might interfere with the SER station at Coulsdon. In addition, the LBSCR agreed to meet the London County Council request that its stretch of line through Cane Hill Asylum grounds should be a covered-way.

Parliament gave the go-ahead for the widening of lines from South Croydon to Redhill in July 1894. The Coulsdon-Redhill section was to be 6 miles 48 chains in length and was described as a new 'avoiding' line (later to be called the Quarry Line). Engineering works were very heavy. Most of the track, much of it parallel to the original SER line, was either in a cutting, on an embankment or in a tunnel. In the Coulsdon area, two bridges were needed to cross and recross the main Brighton Road (A23) and between the bridges the line crossed the Cane Hill Asylum (now Cane Hill Hospital) grounds. The track was located in a cutting which, the Act stipulated, should be temporarily fenced before and during construction. Brick side walls were built which were roofed over and the ground replaced on top. It was not until 1954 that the 'Cane Hill Covered Way' was opened out to save maintenance costs. By this time there were no objections since engine smoke was no longer a problem.

On 5th November 1899 two new stations were opened – Purley Oaks, between South Croydon and Purley, and Stoats Nest (later Coulsdon North). Stoats Nest, a terminus for local trains also incorporating numerous carriage sidings, was conveniently sited just before tracks left to join the new 'avoiding' line. During work on the 'avoiding' line, massive quantities of chalk became available and much of this was needed for

Stoats Nest station which opened in November 1899. Its name was changed to Coulsdon North in June 1911. The station has now closed. (Lens of Sutton)

embankments south of the new Merstham tunnel. Chalk was also used to provide the additional embankments between Croydon and Coulsdon with further amounts being disposed of by filling used gravel pits locally.

Finally the new line from Coulsdon to Earlswood (bypassing Redhill) was ready for use. South of Coulsdon it was officially called the Through Line because with no intermediate stations it was planned that only fast trains would be used. It was not long, however, before it became known as the Quarry Line since at the south end of the new Merstham tunnel, the line ran immediately adjacent to the quarry that had been the southern end of the Croydon, Merstham & Godstone Iron Railway. Although freight traffic began on 5th November 1899, passenger trains could not start until 1st April 1900, by which time three intermediate signal boxes had been completed.

J.T. Howard Turner wrote in his book *The London, Brighton & South Coast Railway: Completion and Maturity* that he had heard on more than one occasion of a connecting passage built

The Gatwick Express travels southwards on the Quarry Line passing where Coulsdon North station once existed. On the right the original 1841 London to Brighton line. (Anthony Rispoli)

Locomotive no 32424 'Beachy Head' Atlantic class 4-4-2 hauls a special RCTS 'Last Atlantic' excursion on 13th April 1958. The train, from Victoria to Newhaven, is seen here leaving Quarry tunnel. The locomotive 'Beachy Head' was built in 1911 and during its life ran 1,090,661 miles. (Arthur Tayler)

Merstham station, c1910. An earlier site in 1841 was considered for use as a junction for trains to Brighton and SER trains to Dover. (Lens of Sutton)

Merstham station almost a century later, photographed in 2002. Merstham remains a busy commuter station on the London to Brighton line. (Anthony Rispoli)

Earlswood station, c1910, where the Quarry Line of 1900 meets the original route through Redhill. (Lens of Sutton)

Horley station, c1901 (before quadrupling), at the original High Street site. A class B4 4-4-0 hauls an express train. (Lens of Sutton)

between the two Merstham tunnels. Had it existed, the passage would have been a steep one for the new tunnel was built about 25 feet higher than the original one and surely the purpose of such a link would need to be questioned anyway. With the tunnels under separate company ownership, the possibility seemed remote.

With the Quarry Line open the LBSCR and SER (now SECR) overcrowding troubles seemed to be resolved. Naturally consideration had already been given to quadrupling track further southwards and to this end authority had been given in August 1899 for widening works between Earlswood and the north end of Balcombe tunnel. Earlswood and Three Bridges stations were extended as required and Horley station was completely rebuilt on a new site to the south of the existing one. The Earlswood to Three Bridges widening came into use in 1907 and the stretch to the Balcombe tunnel junction was opened on 22nd May 1910.

Earlier in 1881, a grisly life or death struggle had taken place in a train as it sped through the Surrey countryside. In fact, had it not been for the sharp eyes of a woman in a cottage not far from the railway line at Horley, a case of murder might well have been difficult to prove. It was by chance she looked out of her window to see two men struggling in a compartment of a passing train.

It was apparently a protracted struggle and by the time the train reached Balcombe tunnel, the victim's body had been bundled out onto the track. At Preston Park a young man staggered from a compartment, covered in blood, saying he had been attacked and robbed. He was taken to Brighton Police Station where it was thought he had attempted suicide.

He returned home to Wallington escorted by a detective (named Holmes!) who saw him to his house to change his clothes. But the young man, whose name was Lefroy, left by a back door. Meanwhile the victim had been found to be Frederick Gold, a 60 year old stockbroker. By now evidence was being collected from the Horley witness and this, with other information, indicated that Lefroy was the murderer. Lefroy was eventually arrested in Stepney by someone claiming a £100 reward and he was found guilty and hanged on 29th November 1881.

18
Branches To Hampton Court, Shepperton And Chessington

LSWR class 1 no 378, built 1903, with passenger set at Hampton Court station, c1910. (Lens of Sutton)

Hampton Court Branch

When Cardinal Wolsey began building Hampton Court Palace on the banks of the Thames in the early 16th century, he little realised that about 450 years later some half million people annually would be arriving at a nearby railway station to view it. When the line first opened on 1st February 1849, horse traction was used, quite a contrast to today's regular electric train service.

An early picture of Hampton Court station building in LSWR days.
(Lens of Sutton)

The branch to Hampton Court left the main line to Woking
west of Surbiton and was less than two miles long. It had little
support from W.J. Chaplin, the LSWR Chairman, when initially
considered but the line went ahead because it was thought 'a
public necessity, affording a fresh means of cheap and legitimate
recreation to the poorer classes'. His doubts were soon dispelled
for by 1865 as many as 13 of the 47 main line departures from
Waterloo were for Hampton Court.

An Act to build the line had been passed on 16th July 1846 but
it was not until January 1848 that work eventually started. The
delay had been caused by financial restrictions due to the
prevailing post-railway mania depression.

There was one intermediate station, at Thames Ditton which
opened in 1851/2 (no precise date recorded). Much of the line
was built on a continuous embankment that levelled off near the
Thames at Hampton Court Bridge. The station, at one time
advertised 'For East and West Molesey', was built of deep red
brick in semi-Jacobean style with decorated windows, corners
and doors plus extravagant gable ends. When services began,

145

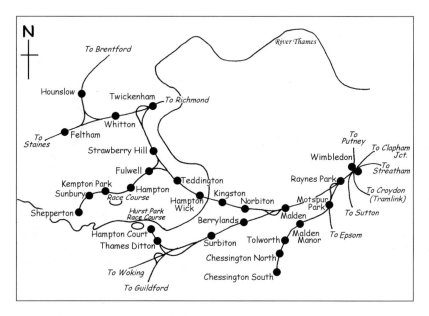

five trains ran each way daily taking about 45 minutes to or from Waterloo.

In July 1915 the Hampton Court flying junction was opened carrying the branch's down line over four main lines. Despite the problems of the First World War, the construction was a considerable achievement with the main girders each 160 feet long and each weighing 85 tons. Third rail electrification to the line from Malden to Hampton Court came one year later in June 1916.

A Branch to Shepperton

In 1861 a company called the Metropolitan & Thames Valley Railway (M&TVR) proposed that a line should be built to connect Isleworth, Richmond, Twickenham and Shepperton via the LSWR and the GWR. A prospectus issued said that London workers 'from the overcrowded and unhealthy portion of the City. ...' should more easily reach healthier localities. Furthermore it was considered that a line to Shepperton should

New Malden, 1st January 2002, where trains leave the main line for Kingston and Shepperton. The station opened as 'Combe and Malden' in 1846. (Anthony Rispoli)

continue to north of Chertsey Bridge to 'capture' traffic from Weybridge but this idea was soon dropped.

Inter-company squabbles ensued with the M&TVR breaking with the GWR over financial matters and turning to the LSWR which in the past had been anxious to keep broad-gauge trains out of the area at any cost. A Shepperton branch was authorised by an Act of 17th July 1862, with the M&TVR now restyled the Thames Valley Railway (TVR). Exactly one year later, agreement was finalised allowing the LSWR to work a proposed single-track line indefinitely in return for expenses and payments to the TVR. In a further development, the TVR and LSWR prepared a joint Bill to extend the branch to Weybridge but the latter decided against this, considering it to be a scheme to poach its main line traffic, and the idea was dropped.

A line from Strawberry Hill to Shepperton opened on 1st November 1864. Initially there were seven passenger trains each way daily and four on Sundays. There was soon agitation to provide a faster service to London and although there was some improvement and more trains provided, the journey still took almost an hour. On 5th July 1865, an Act was passed authorising the LSWR to acquire the company. Attempts still continued locally for the line to be extended to link with the Chertsey branch but without success.

Intermediate stations were Fulwell, Hampton and Sunbury. The line was doubled as far as Fulwell around 1867, but efforts in 1877 to establish a station at Kempton Park near an intended racecourse were refused by the LSWR. Eventually, in September 1878, the LSWR gave way and a private members' platform was provided on the down side. A year later an up platform was approved with the racecourse company paying half the cost. Meanwhile doubling of the track continued with Shepperton reached by 9th December 1878. At Sunbury there were problems when passengers complained in 1886 of (among other things) a nuisance caused by manure traffic! In 1894 a curve was completed which allowed direct running from Shepperton towards Kingston.

The 6½ mile branch line to Shepperton had the distinction of being one of the first to use the new LSWR third rail electric

Teddington (formerly 'Teddington Bushey Park') on the branch from New Malden (formerly Malden) to Twickenham. The line to Shepperton left to the north of the station. Picture taken early 1980s. (J.F. Bradshaw)

Shepperton station photographed 12th September 2001. Close to the station is a Pullman coach 'Malaga' built in 1922 which is today part of Ian Allan Publishing Group's 'Terminal House'. (Anthony Rispoli)

trains. At a time when the LBSCR was going ahead with its 'overhead electrics' (see Chapter 4), LSWR engineer Herbert Jones had visited America with the result that the direct current third rail system was used. Electric trains reached Shepperton on 30th January 1916. Coaches were the usual compartment type with steam coaches having been converted for electric traction. They were made up into three-coach sets with each end-coach having one motor bogie.

It is fitting that on a siding near Shepperton station there is a Pullman car which is today used by the railway book publishers, Ian Allan Ltd. The coach *Malaga* was purchased from the Pullman Car Company in 1963 and it is located on a small section of track adjacent to the company's office building 'Terminal House'. In 1949 the coach was completely refurbished for use by King George VI for journeys on BR Southern Region. It was also used on the Golden Arrow service between Victoria and Dover.

149

Chessington Branch

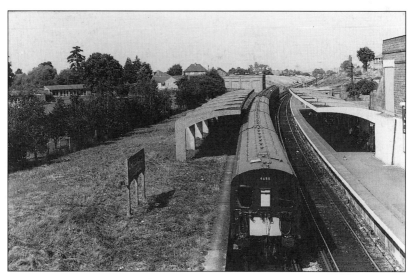

A seven-car unit stops briefly at Chessington South on 3rd August 1964.
The station opened in May 1939. The up platform was never used!
(John H. Meredith)

Chessington branch on the Raynes Park to Epsom line opened
on 28th May 1939, being one of the few to be opened with
electric track. Originally the Southern Railway had intended it
should be a loop leaving the Raynes Park line at Motspur Park
and rejoining the same line north of Leatherhead. Parliamentary
approval had been given in 1930 but by the time Chessington
South had been reached, the threat of war stopped any further
progress southwards and in 1961 the Green Belt scheme stopped
any development south of the now established terminus.

Work on the branch started in 1936 and within two years
Tolworth was reached with an intermediate station at Malden
Manor. Construction had included a 140 ft viaduct over the
Hogsmill River. The remainder of the branch was completed
exactly one year later. Much of the line was built on an embankment and all four stations were constructed mainly of concrete
in what was then considered a futuristic style.

150

Head Codes
denote routes
as under

H HAMPTON COURT

O HOUNSLOW

V TEDDINGTON
& KINGSTON

I CLAYGATE

S SHEPPERTON

The route to health

A picture used in railway compartments which will be remembered by many from the early Southern Electric days where head codes advertised a well-known product. (Photographed courtesy of Hovis Ltd)

The line proved a busy one particularly for travellers to the well-known Chessington Zoo which covered a 65 acre site south of the terminus. Today the site has become the 'Chessington World of Adventure'. It is perhaps less known that the area occupies the site of Burnt Stub, a 14th century house burned down to a 'stub' by Parliamentarians during the Civil War.

The Chessington branch suffered a serious accident in thick fog at the Motspur Park end of the line on 6th November 1947. Due to a signalling error, a train from Holmwood ran into the side of a busy evening Waterloo to Chessington South commuter train as it crossed onto the branch. Four passengers were killed and a number injured.

Chessington branch line was the last to be constructed by Sir Herbert Walker's Southern Railway and when built in the late 1930s it was considered to be a 'line of the future'.

Conclusion

The decline of many Surrey lines commenced during the 1920s. Buses were on the increase providing a more flexible service than the trains. In addition, road haulage was on the increase. Yet unlike its neighbouring counties, Surrey has to date suffered relatively few line closures.

The county's main loss was in June 1965 when the branch from Horsham to Guildford closed. With bus services available throughout the area, the line no longer served a useful purpose. A short branch from Woodside to Selsdon closed in May 1983. With passenger traffic having continually decreased over the years, the line could hardly be justified. Further closures came more recently on 31st May 1997 when the short branch to Addiscombe and the line from West Croydon to Wimbledon both came to an end to make way for the construction of Croydon Tramlink.

A major factor contributing to the decline of the railways during the 20th century was the elimination of competition between private companies brought about by 'grouping' in 1923. This had the effect of merging more than 100 existing companies throughout Great Britain into four main companies: LNER (London & North Eastern Railway); LMS (London Midland & Scottish Railway); GWR (Great Western Railway); and SR (Southern Railway).

Meantime changes were taking place which were to materially affect the railways and their future. With living standards rising and paid holidays becoming the norm, people were willing to live further from their place of work. Electricity was becoming more freely available and, with the coalfields of the North no longer vital to industry, people were migrating southwards. The Home Counties became a popular area and the need arose to provide extensive suburban rail services between the capital and the surrounding districts.

It was in this climate that the Southern Railway developed its electric services. An AC overhead system had already been inherited from its predecessors, the LBSCR, providing services as far south as Coulsdon North and Sutton. In 1926, the present DC system was adopted and by 1928, 'third rail' electrics were installed along the old SER lines to Caterham and Tattenham Corner. Eventually, threatened by effective coach and motorcar competition between London and Brighton, electric trains were provided to the coast. During the next few years, electrification extended rapidly throughout much of the network to be halted only when the Second World War began.

The war effectively wrecked the finances of the railways which were to be saved by nationalisation in 1948. With Government subsidies involved it was inevitable that 'rationalisation' processes would follow. Management of the main line railways was delegated by the British Transport Commission to the Railway Executive with the Southern Region taking charge of all lines in the South. But progress to commence capital investment programmes was slow due to material shortages. In addition integration with other forms of transport, a declared aim of nationalisation, made little headway.

In 1953 there were changes. A Transport Act aimed at decentralisation dissolved the Railway Executive and from January 1955 the Southern Region was controlled by a Board, responsible to the Commission, but with considerable freedom to determine its own actions. Three Divisions were created, the 'South Eastern', 'South Western' and 'Central'. Whereas the SECR and the LSWR had to some extent regained their old titles, the Board regretted that neither 'Brighton' nor 'South Coast' from the LBSCR could be included.

Despite optimistic plans for redevelopment, freight traffic was on the decline and the railways were becoming more dependent on passenger traffic. By the early 1960s, the Government's attitude had hardened. In a further Transport Act of 1962, it was clear that commercial viability was considered a more important factor than providing a service to the public. In 1963 the Transport Commission was dissolved and a new Railways Board created. At the same time, the Minister of Transport appointed the Stedeford Group to look at the future of the railways. The findings were not published but one of its members was Dr Richard Beeching (later Lord Beeching), a name that was to become very well known in the years to come.

Proposals were made in a report which became popularly known as the 'Beeching Plan'. Basically the idea was to keep lines considered suitable to rail traffic and give up the remainder. It had been calculated that one third of the rail system in Britain carried only 1% of the total traffic! The report was considered disappointing in ignoring the potential of many Southern lines, particularly related to electrification. Also by planning the closure of many freight depots, it was thought the report failed to foresee the future of container traffic in the region. Line singling, 'bus-stop' type stations for economy and the use of diesel-electric locomotives were other aspects considered overlooked at the time.

It is difficult at the present time to foresee the railway's future. One of the main disadvantages is that its future is in the hands of politicians. Sadly the days have gone when the railways provided an efficient service throughout and when railway employees could take a real pride in the job.

Opening and Final Closure Dates of Lines

Line	Opened	Final Closure
Surrey Iron Railway		
Wandsworth to Croydon*	1803	1846
Mitcham to Hackbridge*	1804	1846
Croydon, Merstham & Godstone Iron Railway*	1805	1839
Brookwood to Necropolis Cemetery	1854	1941
West Croydon to Wimbledon	1855	1997
Elmers End to Addiscombe	1864	1997
Horsham to Guildford	1865	1965
Woodside to Selsdon	1885	1983
Brookwood to Bisley Camp	1890	1952

* These 'railways' were built with flanged rails mounted on stone blocks with wagons drawn by horses, donkeys or mules.

Bibliography

In compiling *Lost Railways of Surrey*, I have referred to numerous sources, many now out of print, which include the following and which can be recommended for further reading:

Bayliss, Derek *Retracing the First Public Railway* (Living History Publications, Croydon)

Body, Geoffrey *Railways of the Southern Region* (Patrick Stephens Ltd)

Course, Dr Edwin *The Railways of Southern England* and *Independent and Light Railways* (B.T. Batsford Ltd)

Dendy Marshall, C.F. revised by Kidner, R.W. *History of the Southern Railway* (Ian Allan Ltd)

Gray, Adrian *The Railways of Mid-Sussex* and *The London to Brighton Line* (Oakwood Press)

Hadfield, Charles *The Canals of South and South East England* (David & Charles)

Hamilton Ellis, C. *The London, Brighton & South Coast Railway* (Ian Allen Ltd)

Harding, Peter A. & Clarke, John M. *The Bisley Camp Branch Line* (Peter A. Harding, Woking)

Herbert, W.B. *Railway Ghosts* (David & Charles)

Hodd, H.R. *The Horsham-Guildford Direct Railway* (Oakwood Press)

King, John & Tait, Geoffrey *Golden Gatwick* (Royal Aeronautical Society, Gatwick Branch, and the BAA)

Kirby, J.R.W. *The Banstead and Epsom Downs Railway* (Oakwood Press)

Mitchell, Vic & Smith, Keith *Southern Main Lines, Epsom to Horsham; Horsham & Guildford Direct Railway* (Middleton Press)

Owen, N. *The Tattenham Corner Branch* (Oakwood Press)

Salter, Brian J. *Epsom Town, Downs and Common* (Living History Publications, Croydon)

Spence, Jeoffry *Caterham through the Centuries* from *Caterham & Warlingham – Jubilee History* (The Bourne Society)
The Caterham Railway (Oakwood Press)

Turner, J.T Howard *The London, Brighton & South Coast Railway: Origins and Formations; Establishment and Growth; Completion and Maturity* (B.T. Batsford Ltd)

White, H.P. *Forgotten Railways South East England A Regional History of the Railways of Great Britain, Vol 2: Southern England* (David & Charles)

Williams, R.A. *The London & South Western Railway, Vol 1 The Formative Years; Vol 2 Growth and Consolidation* (David & Charles)

Index

INDEX

Epsom Downs Extension Company 128
Epsom Downs Extension Railway 128
Epsom Racecourse 100–105
Ewell 35

Farnborough 56, 68
Farnham 50, 52
Forest Hill 32, 34, 35, 38
Fulwell 148

Gatwick 11, 57, 61, 62, 93, 122–126
Gatwick Express 126, 140
Gatwick Racecourse 93, 122–125
Godalming 56
Godstone 15, 16, 17, 65, 66, 67, 78, 83
Godstone Road (Purley) 77, 79, 129
Gomshall 57
Great Eastern Railway (GER) 31
Great Western Railway (GWR) 50, 55, 56, 65,
  146, 147, 152
Groombridge 115, 117
Guildford 10, 48–54, 55, 56, 106 seq, 152
Guildford Junction Company 48, 50

Hackbridge 13, 15
Halliloo Platform 77
Hampton 148
Hampton Court 144–146
  junction 50
Haywards Heath 30, 40, 64, 131, 135
Holmwood 88, 89, 110, 151
Hooley 15, 17
Horley 40, 41, 122, 124, 142, 143
Horsham 10, 50, 85, 88, 106 seq, 152
Horsham & Guildford Direct Railway
  Company 107
Horsham, Dorking & Leatherhead company
  88
Hurst Green 118, 119

Kempton Park 148
Kenley 79, 83
Kingston 100, 147, 148
Kingswood and Burgh Heath 128 seq

Leatherhead 59, 85 seq
Lingfield 115, 119, 121
Locomotive Club of Great Britain (LCGB)
  63, 82, 112
London & Brighton Electric Railway 40, 63
London & Brighton Railway (L&BR) 16, 18,
  21–31, 34, 36, 63, 64, 77 seq, 84 seq, 101,
  134, 137, 153
London & Croydon Railway (L&CR) 10, 11,
  20–26, 34, 36, 84

London & Greenwich Railway (L&GR) 11,
  20–21
London & North Eastern Railway (LNER)
  152
London & North Western Railway (LNWR)
  19, 31
London & Southampton Railway 100
London & South Western Railway (LSWR)
  11, 21, 26, 41, 50, 52, 54, 55, 68 seq, 84 seq,
  101, 107, 144 seq, 153
London, Brighton and Shoreham Pneumatic
  Conveyance Co 33
London, Brighton & South Coast Railway
  (LBSCR) 11, 18, 26, 36 seq, 40 seq, 50, 56,
  59, 65, 93 seq, 100 seq, 107 seq, 114 seq, 125,
  128 seq, 149, 153
London, Chatham & Dover Railway (LCDR)
  127, 129
London, Midland & Scottish Railway (LMS)
  19, 152
London Necropolis Company (LNC) 69–71
London to Brighton 9, 11, 32, 33, 39, 40, 46,
  63, 96, 114, 117, 122, 124, 135, 140, 153

Malden (see also New Malden) 146
Malden Manor 150
Marden Park 118
Merstham 9, 12 seq, 137, 141
  tunnel 47, 135, 137, 139, 143
Merton Abbey 29, 30
Metropolitan & Brighton Railway 80
Metropolitan & Thames Valley Railway
  (M&TVR) 146–147
Mickleham tunnel 86
Mitcham 13, 18, 29
  Junction 26, 43
Motspur Park 47, 150, 151

Necropolis branch line 10, 68–71
New Addington 25
New Beckenham 91, 94
New Cross 34, 36, 37, 91, 94, 117
New Cross Gate 21, 94
New Croydon 30–31
New Malden (formerly Malden) 147, 148

North Camp 57
Northwood 89
Norwood 26, 34, 35, 43, 134
Nutfield 66

Ockley 88, 89, 110
Oxted 47, 65, 66, 93, 94, 114–121, 129

Park Hill tunnel 94

159

Peasmarsh 56
Pirbright 74–75
Portsmouth 9, 16, 34, 48, 56, 57
Portsmouth Railway 56
Prosser, William (Prosser's system) 49, 50
Purley 77 seq, 101, 128 seq
Purley Oaks 138

Quarry Line 46, 138–143
Quarry tunnel 140

Railway Correspondence and Travel Society
(RCTS) 75, 112, 140
Raynes Park 101, 150
Reading 10, 50, 55 seq, 64, 67, 130
Reading, Guildford & Reigate Company 55
Redhill (see also Reigate) 40, 46, 50, 55 seq,
63 seq, 78, 82, 115, 116, 129, 134 seq
Reedham Halt 130, 131
Reigate (see also Redhill) 9, 15, 46, 55 seq, 78,
134
Riddlesdown 118
Royal Train 104, 131
Rudgwick 106, 108

St Catherine's tunnel 50
Salfords Halt 46
Sanderstead 97, 117–118, 129
Selhurst 43
Selsdon 10, 65, 91, 94 seq 114 seq, 152
Shalford 55 seq
Shepley Mills 13, 15
Shepperton 146–149
Slinfold 108
Smitham 130
South Croydon 30, 46, 94, 96, 115, 117, 131,
138
South Eastern & Chatham Railway (SECR)
94, 97, 129, 143, 153
South Eastern Railway (SER) 10, 11, 21, 34,
50, 52, 55–62, 63–67, 78–83, 88, 93 seq, 114
seq, 129, 134, 137 seq, 153
Southern Counties Touring Society (SCTS)
24, 30
Southern Electric 44, 47, 151
Southern Heights Light Railway 118
Southern Railway (SR) 19, 45, 46, 59, 65, 66,
90, 118, 151, 152
South Western & Epsom Junction Railway
101

Spencer Road Halt 97
Stoats Nest (see also Coulsdon North) 78,
101, 128, 130, 138–139
Strawberry Hill 147
Sunbury 148
Surbiton (formerly Kingston) 100
Surrey & Sussex Junction Railway (S&SJR)
114–115
Surrey Iron Railway (SIR) 9, 11, 12–18, 19,
26, 31
Sutton 34, 35, 39, 43, 45, 46, 100 seq, 128, 153

Tadworth 128, 131
Tattenham Corner 127–133, 153
Teddington 148
Thames Ditton 145
Thames Valley Railway (TVR) 147
Three Bridges 46, 60, 67, 85, 88, 143
Tinsley Green 122, 124, 125
Tolworth 150
Tonbridge 10, 60, 62, 63 seq, 78, 83, 115 seq
Tongham 10, 51, 52–54, 57
Tulse Hill 42
Tunbridge Wells 114 seq
Twickenham 148

Uckfield 118, 119
Upper Warlingham 118

Waddon Marsh 18, 27, 28
Wallington (formerly Carshalton) 34
Wanborough 52, 57
Wandsworth 9, 12 seq, 26, 41
Warlingham 79, 81
Warnham 88
West Croydon 10, 13, 18, 20 seq, 32 seq, 43,
84, 101, 152
West End Terminus (Bricklayer's Arms) 21
West London Railway 34
Weybridge 147
Whyteleafe 77, 79, 81, 118
Willesden Junction 31
Wimbledon 10, 13, 18, 25, 26 seq, 46, 68, 84,
99, 152
Woking 48, 50, 68 seq, 145
Woldingham 118
Woodmansterne 131
Woodside 10, 65, 91–99, 114 seq, 122, 152
tunnel 91, 94
Woodside and South Croydon company 94